Reincarnation

The Ultimate Guide to Rebirth, Karma and Old Souls and What Astrology, Wicca and Other Spiritual Practices Say About Past Lives

Your Free Gift (only available for a limited time)

Thanks for getting this book! If you want to learn more about various spirituality topics, then join Mari Silva's community and get a free guided meditation MP3 for awakening your third eye. This guided meditation mp3 is designed to open and strengthen ones third eye so you can experience a higher state of consciousness. Simply visit the link below the image to get started.

https://spiritualityspot.com/meditation

Contents

Introduction

Reincarnation, rebirth, or transmigration, whatever the term, the concept of life after death has been around for thousands of years. The ideas surrounding this concept are just as compelling today as they were in ancient history. We all have an idea of what happens to us when we die, but nobody knows for sure.

Why do some people believe in reincarnation, and some refuse to entertain the idea? Cultural and religious influences can play a part, but so can lack of knowledge and failing to understand how the process works. Other books may claim to answer all your questions but then focus on one idea. This book is an easy-to-understand guide written to help you consider all the different cultural beliefs and how you can explore your past lives.

Do you know someone who is an old soul or who seems wise beyond their years? Is that how people describe you? Take a quiz to discover if you are indeed an old soul who has lived many lives before the one you are currently living. Discover if you have karmic baggage holding you back and learn how to deal with it.

You may believe in reincarnation, or you may be a skeptic, but this book has something for everyone and is packed with practical methods and instructions to help you find the answers to many questions about life after death and reincarnation.

If you are curious to discover if you lived in Ancient Rome as a gladiator or if you served in the Court of King Arthur in your past lives, then read on. The answers may surprise you!

Chapter 1: What is Reincarnation?

The afterlife, life after death, transmigration, or metempsychosis - call it what you will - is something most religions and belief systems have something to say about the concept of reincarnation. Consider natural life and the cyclical route it takes. Night follows day, seasons follow each other and form a yearly cycle, and nature shows us amazing rebirths every day. Seeds that come from dying plants are planted and reborn, often more robust and more developed.

Reincarnation is the concept that the soul or some aspect of our self is reborn and evolved. Our soul matures and learns from the mistakes it has made in past lives. The concept is based on the belief that if we keep dying feeling unfulfilled, we will continue to return until we reach our final liberation.

Reincarnation is thought to happen to individuals who believe in the process and seek the spirituality that accompanies the process. Not all souls require fulfillment. Some individuals live a life filled with experiences firmly rooted in their present lives, and they won't feel the need to mature. Others will spend time in the present seeking answers that will help them define their sense of self and realize the need for a journey of self-realization.

Reincarnation and its Impact on the Scientific World

While most scientific studies are designed to deal with worldly matters, one scientist decided to explore the potential that reincarnation is real. In Virginia, he founded the Division of Perceptual studies and formed a team to study the evidence of former lives, near-death experiences, and other related phenomena.

Dr. Ian Stevenson worked for over four decades investigating reincarnation stories, and he published many articles and books on the subject. While he refused to state the absolute plausibility of reincarnation, his work did suggest that it was possible. He stated that if possible, he would attempt to communicate after his death. He bought a lock and set it with a mnemonic code. He is believed to have told colleagues he would pass on the mnemonic code after his death so they could open the lock. Since his death in 2007, the lock has remained closed.

Stevenson's work was mainly with children who seemed to have unexplained memories of a former life, and he made some startling connections with his subjects and their supposed former existences. He coined the phrase "the survival of personality after death" to describe reincarnation and saw the condition as a possible explanation for the emergence of gender dysphoria, antipathy, and other unexplained personality traits.

Reincarnation is derived from Latin and means "entering the flesh again." There are many cases in both adults and children that provide evidence it happens. Dr. Michael Newton, Ph.D., was a leading expert in the field and founded the Newton Institute in 2002 to study the life between lives. He developed hypnotic regression techniques still used today and was considered a pioneer in his field. With Dr. Stevenson, they provide compelling evidence of over 3,000 cases of reincarnation that proved the theory.

The Stages of Death

The steps below indicate the research the doctors carried out about what happens following death. They have been gathered from subjects with memories of their death in a former life or have undergone successful regression and describe the process they remember.

Death

Most reports begin with the sensation of looking down on their own body and seeing people mourning them. The subjects report the feeling of frustration at the inability to talk to the living as they leave the room. There is a sense of being pulled as a bright light illuminates the mouth of a tunnel.

Once they reach the light, there is a succession of positive influences ready to greet them. These can be relatives who have already passed or visions of scenery. Most subjects report that music is played as they move to the mouth of the tunnel and prepare to pass through.

Subjects now describe the decision they must make. One of the beings who greets them will ask, "Are you ready to die?" If the subject says, "Yes, I am ready to die," then the silver cord that attaches them to their Earthly body is cut and drifts away from them. If the answer is "No, I'm not ready to die," they will be sent back to the physical world to arrive seconds before they would have died.

This form of return is generally described as a near miss, an NDE experience, or a miracle recovery. It may seem a haphazard way to organize death, but subjects report the decision is an easy one to make. If they feel the time is right, they will move on, or if they feel they have things to do, they will return. Most subjects report staying around their relatives and friends until the funeral.

Healing

This stage is not always part of the process, but some subjects have experienced it. They describe a "shower of light" bathing their soul as they let go of any regrets, trauma, and negativity from their previous life and reform in a vibrant way.

The Review

This stage is described as taking place in a library setting with a panel of wise ones or elders. At this stage, souls that are less evolved than others meet with their allotted guides and make amends and heal through reincarnation. More evolved souls can spend months or even years in this stage as they review their past lives and decide their next step. These reviews are described as positive experiences free from judgment with loving and kind souls eager to help.

The Reunion

This is when the soul meets with its soul family. These can be souls who connect with us in life and have passed on or can be members of our family. At the reunion, the soul family will compare experiences and learn from the information they absorb.

Life Selection

This stage marks the beginning of the regeneration process. Most subjects describe the setting as like a large cinema with multiple screens. The soul is then shown multiple paths it can choose from when it returns to Earth. A fast-forward function enables the soul to consider the whole experience of each timeline, gaining greater perspective on the path it follows.

Our spirituality and intellect will always choose a path that is rewarding and sets challenges. Souls who have shown interest in specific fields will choose to pick up where they left off in their previous life. Musical talents, sports excellence, and artistic talents are still with us when we are born. This explains how child prodigies and other hugely talented children are formed.

Preparation

This stage is the penultimate stage before reincarnation. Subjects report meeting souls who will feature in their new life and form plans to meet when the time is right. Guides help the subject implant symbols in their perception that will trigger them to perform certain actions or meet with other souls at specific times.

This synchronization leads to the meetings we often describe as "a meeting of minds" or "meeting your soul mates." These connections are immediate and can be triggered by different stimuli. These cues are all pre-programmed and should be acted on.

Rebirth

Subjects will often report traveling back to Earth along the same tunnel from which they departed. The pull will bring them back to Earth and straight into their mother's womb. This is when most people experience amnesia and appear to start life with a clean slate. Some people may question why there is a need to forget what has happened in former lives and cast off our true origins.

The answer seems to be that if we remembered every detail of our former lives, then we wouldn't feel the need to learn in our next life. Imagine sitting a test with the answers already in your head. This is why we have soul families and spiritual guides to help us face the experiences ahead with a strong resolve.

This veil of illusion theory also explains why memories of former lives are often more vivid in children under 5. They will remember details and experiences from another existence that can be troubling for them, and they may feel uncomfortable for a while. Some children will manifest these memories as imaginary friends who represent the people they left behind.

Compelling Reincarnation Stories

The best evidence is the recollections of subjects who have seemingly been through the process. Here are some of the most interesting cases of reincarnation and past life experiences.

Bruce Whittier

This is a case of an American man having recurrent dreams about being a Jewish man hiding in his family home alongside his family. His dreams contained images of a clock, and he drew a picture in great detail when he woke. His rabbi questioned him about his experiences, and Bruce told him the name of the Jewish man was Stefan Horowitz, a Dutch Jew who perished along with his family at Auschwitz.

Following the discussion, Whittier had a dream about the location of the clock in an antique shop. He traveled to the location in his dream and saw the clock in the window. The dealer informed him that the clock had been imported from the Netherlands as part of a retired German Major's belongings. This was the final piece of the puzzle for Whittier, who became convinced of his past life.

Gus Taylor

As an 18-month infant, Gus began to talk about the fact he was his own grandad. He became enthralled by family photos and pointed out pictures of his "Grandpa Augie" at an early age. The defining fact for the family was when Gus began to talk about his dead sister, who had disappeared when he was young. This was a family secret that Gus couldn't possibly have known about. His grandpa, Augie's sister, was killed and dumped in the San Francisco Bay.

When asked about how he remembered his former life, Gus told his family that God had given him a ticket back to Earth. He described traveling through a long tunnel and landing in his mommy's belly. This was when he came back as Gus with memories of being

Augie. The timeline seemed to fit as Gus's grandpa had died a year before Gus was born.

Reincarnation in Hollywood

This story is possibly one of the best-known examples of reincarnation and its effects on children. In 2005 in Oklahoma, Ryan Hammons was born to Baptist parents with everyday jobs. In 2009, young Ryan began to role play as a movie director despite his family having no connection to the industry.

He told his mom tales of Hollywood and described living in a huge white house with a swimming pool on the street with the word "rock" in its name. He told her he had been married five times and had three sons and a daughter. His mom dismissed his stories as fanciful and even kept them from his dad.

Things changed when she started to believe her son and began to look for evidence. She got books from the local library about Hollywood and went through them with her son. One picture from the 1932 movie "Night After Night," starring Mae West, changed her mind completely. The shot included a group of men wearing hats and overcoats, and Ryan reacted to it strongly. "Hey Mom," he yelled, "that's me, and that's George. We did a film together," pointing at the man in the middle of the shot, and the guy stood next to him.

Ryan's mom decided to get professional help and called on Dr. Jim Tucker to see her son. Dr. Tucker was a well-known child psychologist who dealt with past live cases in children. He questioned Ryan and recorded detailed accounts of the man who had been in the photo, Marty Martin, and his life in Hollywood. When asked how he died, Ryan described his heart exploding, and Dr. Tucker confirmed that Marty had died from a heart attack in 1964.

When the family traced Marty's daughter, she confirmed 55 separate details that Ryan had given about his previous life. He described dancing with Rita Hayworth and lavish Hollywood parties that Marty attended with elaborate details. As Ryan aged, his memories faded, and at 11, he became a typical boy with regular thoughts of baseball and school rather than Hollywood parties and film stars.

Ruth Simmons

In 1956, a film was made called "The Search for Bridey Murphy" that explored Ruth Simmons's experience and connection to 19th century Ireland. In 1952, Ruth underwent hypnotic regression therapy with her therapist, which led to her speaking in a heavy Irish accent. She told stories of her life in Belfast and the poverty she endured during her lifetime. While her stories were detailed, they lacked details that could be verified until she mentioned her food suppliers. Ruth said that Bridey got her supplies from Mr. Carrigan and Mr. Farr. Researchers obtained the town directory for the years she described and found the two names listed as grocers.

The Indian Businessman

Parmod Sharma was born in Bisauli, India, in 1944. At two, he was already different from other boys in the village. He berated his mother for cooking and suggested that she let his wife in Moradabad do it instead. He told his parents he was a successful businessman who had run shops selling cookies and water. He made cookies with mud and constructed miniature shops to sell them from.

He described a life much more opulent than the one his parents lived and warned them of the dangers of eating curd. He talked about a family business called Mohan Brothers that was successful in Mahabad. Parmod also disliked bathing and would panic and claim he had died in a bathtub when placed in one.

Eventually, Parmod's parents relented and journeyed with their son the 145km to Moradabad to discover the truth. They discovered that there had been a family living at the address Parmod had supplied called Mehra, who operated a family business called Mohan Brothers. The business was a successful soft drink and cookie shop, and it was managed by Parmanand Mehra, who had passed away in 1943. Details of his death emerged and shocked the Sharma family. Parmanand had overeaten curd, which caused him to have gastric problems, and was prescribed medicinal baths as a cure. It was believed that he had taken a bath directly before his demise.

Dilukshi Nisanka

In Sri Lanka, a belief in reincarnation is not unusual, but it is the home of one of the most credible cases that prove it exists. Dilukshi frequently spoke about her previous life and insisted that her parents were not her true family as she had parents elsewhere in a place called Dambulla. She spoke of her death at six, falling from a bridge and drowning.

Her parents were troubled by her insistencies, and they repeated their story to a local reporter who published their story in a newspaper article. The family was amazed to receive a letter just weeks later from a man who claimed his daughter Shiromi was reincarnated as Dilukshi. He told the family that her story matched the details of his daughter's death, and the two families arranged to meet.

The Nisanka family traveled 145km to meet the family and see what happened. Once Dilukshi reached the family dwelling at Dambulla, she appeared entirely at ease with the family and chatted away with them as if she had known them forever. The facts she told them about Shiromi matched completely, and Dilukshi was interested in visiting local spots she had enjoyed in her former life.

Jenny Cockell

This is the story of an ordinary housewife living in Northampton, England. Her story started when she was four years old, and she remembered her past life as Mary Sutton, who lived in Ireland. She never mentioned her experiences and the small snatches of information she felt to anyone because she believed everybody had the same feelings about past lives. As she got older, she felt sorrow about her former life and described her death giving birth to her eighth child. One day she felt drawn to a map of Ireland and was drawn to a place called Malahide.

Life went on for Jenny, and she became a mother herself, but the feelings never left her. In fact, they strengthened, and she decided to track down Mary's family in Ireland. As a pragmatic Christian whose belief system didn't include reincarnation, she decided to take a skeptical stance about the whole process. She underwent a series of regression sessions to make sure she got the details right. She drew detailed maps of Malahide and compared them to actual maps of the area. The details were astonishingly accurate, and this spurred her to visit the town and track down Mary's family.

Once she arrived in Dublin, Jenny got to work checking out church records and researching the Sutton family line. She quickly discovered that Mary had lived and died in the Malahide area, and her eight surviving children had been placed with relatives or sent to the orphanage. Realizing what a huge task she had before her, Jenny contacted the local newspapers and churches for help.

Finally, in 1990, Jenny spoke to Sonny Sutton by telephone. He was the first of Mary's children to make contact, and he was impressed by the conversation. He told his siblings that he genuinely believed he had just spoken with his mother. The rest of the family were less convinced and needed more proof. They eventually met with Jenny and were amazed at the details she knew about them and their former home.

Perhaps the most convincing part of the story lies with Jenny. She is a MENSA member and a very down-to-earth typical British housewife who couldn't possibly have fabricated any part of this story. Whatever your beliefs, there is no doubt that this story is remarkable.

Do the stories here prove that reincarnation exists? Maybe, maybe not. The choice is yours.

Chapter 2: Buddhism vs. Judaism

Traditionally reincarnation is based on an original soul being reborn into different bodies and becoming a mature soul that will eventually enter the spiritual realm as a completed entity. The Jewish faith has different beliefs. Their ideas are more complicated and involve beliefs far from mainstream.

The Jewish Beliefs About Reincarnation

The esoteric part of Judaism is known as Kabballah and teaches us that the soul is divided into five parts that each play a role in the human psyche's makeup. Two of these parts remain in the Heavenly realm while the other three accompany you on Earth, and you can work directly with them to improve your status.

Chayah: The World of Emanation

Meaning living essence, this is part of the soul with little connection with the physical body. It resides in the ether and is rarely part of consciousness until the soul ascends into Heaven. It represents the state of awareness that signifies the experience of the ultimate Jewish enlightenment. Judaism credits the chayah as the dimension where mankind can merge with God and become part of a pure oneness.

Yehida: The World of Will

Judaism teaches us that yehida is the central part of the soul kept in the infinitude of creation. It doesn't accompany the mortal soul to Earth, as it is considered the most connected source of awareness. Some consider the yehida to be the direct line to God and the essence of the Divine region. Jewish people call on their yehida to give them the awareness to cope with difficult Earthly experiences.

Nefesh: The World of Action

This is the level of the soul most connected with physicality. It is sometimes called the animal soul and is present in every particle of matter on the Earthly plane. Every blade of grass, particle of soil, and even single-cell amoeba are credited with this aspect of the soul.

As humans, the nefesh is the aspect of the soul associated with physical awareness. You are born with the nefesh, and it is often described as your life force or will to live. When you leave the physical world, your nefesh will linger around your body for the longest time and ensure that it is purified correctly following death. The mystical thought of Kaballah is represented by books known as the Zohar, which describe the nefesh as the dark part of the candle flame that clings to the wick. It links the nefesh with the next soul level, the ruach, and explains that when both parts of the soul are enlightened, they provide a throne for the highest level, the neshama, to form a complete light.

The nefesh is considered the densest part of the soul that forms a cornerstone for the other two levels that accompany humans on Earth.

Ruach: The World of Information

Meaning wind or spirit, this is the part of the soul associated with the senses or emotions. It forms the basis of spirituality and will move humans to tears at just a momentary glance of beauty. The ruach is nourished by experiences and will be affected by the way we live our lives.

Neshema: The World of Creation

Meaning breath, this part of the soul is the defining quality of human consciousness. The power of neshema can be nourished only by people who seek to live pure lives. Consider the ruach and the nefesh as the body's fuels, while the neshema is the higher level of the soul that allows communication with the higher being. Simply put, human existence is lacking if the soul has not been lit by the celestial light that emits from the neshema.

Fixing your soul is not an easy task.

Judaism teaches that fixing your soul means all five levels need to perfect, so that would seem to suggest five lifetimes minimum. Think again. Each level of the soul is split into five levels, making a total of twenty-five spiritual levels. If one level of spirituality is completed during every lifetime, that means at least twenty-five lifetimes is needed. Spiritually speaking, that would be quite an achievement. The second principle of Jewish reincarnation is that you will need numerous tries to fix your soul, and it cannot all be done in a few lifetimes.

God will give you 1,000 lifetimes to get it right.

Providing you are on the right path, Jewish people believe that you have 1,000 different lifetimes to get your soul to the higher level it needs to be at. If you think this sounds like a chance to mess about on Earth and leave the healing of your soul until later, then think again. If you aren't fixing your soul levels from the first time on Earth, you will receive only two more chances. If you fail to improve after three lifetimes, God will split your soul into its multiple components and redistribute them to others.

There are no new souls on Earth.

Judaism believes that at this stage of history, everyone on Earth is an "old" soul. This could explain why modern life is so confusing, and the need for spiritual healing has never been so high. It is believed that because every soul on Earth is now made up of non-rectified parts of souls from history, many spiritual loose ends need to be tied up.

Purgatory is not concerned with Earthly misdemeanors.

Jewish purgatory is often compared with the Christian concept named Hell. This is not correct. Purgatory is the Jewish faith's place of atonement for people who committed sins against God on Earth. For instance, if someone didn't follow the commandments on Earth, they will be taken to task in purgatory and must pay the price. If someone committed more Earthly sins like theft or violence against others, they would pay in the next life.

Reincarnation helps you correct the mistakes you made in your former life. You may have treated your partner badly in your last life, so you probably will find yourself in a relationship where your life is made to feel like hell. Reincarnation could answer the question, "Why do bad things happen to good people?"

Nobody suffers for no reason.

Judaism believes the soul is meant to atone for your past mistakes. Take Job as an example. He is often seen as the biblical prototype for undeserved suffering. He was a seemingly good man who Satan beset. He lost his home, his family, and his health, although he could live. So why was Job so tormented when he seemed to be the poster boy for all that was holy?

The ancient Jewish midrash or textual interpretation of the Talmud explains that Job was the reincarnation of Terah, Abraham's father. Terah led a pagan life and served as an idolatrous priest, peddling his wicked idols in a shop before Abraham chased them away. This led to Abraham being cast into a fiery furnace to perish, but God saved him. This was when Terah regretted his former actions and committed to living a righteous life with no reward. When he was reincarnated as Job, this was his chance to show God he wouldn't waver in his beliefs no matter how much he had to suffer.

Kabbalistic Literature Mentions Three Types of Reincarnation

1) Gilgul: The Hebrew word for rolling. This is transmigration proper. Gilgul is the purest form of reincarnation when one body's soul is sent back to Earth to inhabit another body. This form of reincarnation can occur between different species and is not restricted to humans.

2) Ibbur: This form of reincarnation is trickier. It involves the soul of another descending from Heaven to enter the physical body of someone already alive. This is a form of possession when God believes the human subject needs assistance and sends a mature soul to assist them for a given time.

3) Dybbuk: This is a less acceptable form of reincarnation and has only been recognized as a late concept in Jewish history. This form of reincarnation refers to tortured souls, often pursued by devils, entering a body on Earth to seek solace and rest. Removing this form of possession would mean exorcism.

Many Jewish scholars treat the subject of reincarnation with care. They see the concept as dangerous and take the view it can taint their pure religious ideals. The Talmud has no references to transmigration, and the idea is thought to have entered Judaism in the eighth century via Greek, Indian, and other Gnostic religious influences.

Buddhism and Reincarnation

There are a lot of misconceptions about Buddhism and reincarnation. These misunderstandings arise because we are incapable of interpreting the sacred sutras and writings set down by the Buddha. After all, life has moved on. It is reported that he left 84,000 teachings that represented the diverse characteristics of humanity. He preached his doctrine depending on the mental and spiritual level of his audience.

Teachers and scholars used the idea of reincarnation to instill fear into the simple villagers to whom they were preaching. The idea of returning to Earth in animal form would have frightened them into behaving better in their current life. The doctrine of reincarnation was used as a powerful tool to teach morality.

Modern life is different, and the parables used in the time of Buddha are largely irrelevant, yet many Buddhists in the East and West persist in believing in individual reincarnation. True Buddhism is based on the belief that no part of our true self survives death. The core of Buddhism is that all beings are constantly in a state of flux. We are always changing, learning, and then dying. Leaving behind the physical realm and the energies, we have taken a new form and transmigrate from one life to the next. This is known as rebirth and the sense of self living on as another life.

This is not an easy concept to understand, and there are schools of Buddhism dedicated to teaching its followers how to recognize the illusions of self and how to liberate themselves from this illusion.

Some Buddhists believe that the Tibetan teaching aid "The Wheel of Life" and the Ten Spiritual Realms within the doctrine suggest that some form of reincarnation is necessary to progress. This is not the same concept as the traditional thoughts on reincarnation that have a different understanding in other religions like Hinduism.

What are the ten spiritual realms of Buddhism?

According to the cosmology of Buddhism, these realms refer to ten states of mind. Four of these realms are related to the evolution of consciousness, and the other six are inferior and related to reactions to external forces. The first four superior states are influenced by teachings, self-improvement, and the desire to discover inner strength.

Buddhahood

This is the highest of the ten realms. This is a state of enlightenment and inner peace that identifies Buddhists who have reached the top ranks of the religion. This state is also known as the state of Buddha and is a mark of nobility within the religion.

Bodhisattva

This is the state of mind in which the mind reaches a level of altruism and compassion. When the mind reaches this state, it is consumed by the desire to help others and free the world from suffering. In this state, your whole life is dedicated to selflessness and kindness. You will find your compassion levels will give you the highest level of satisfaction, and helping others will lead to inner peace.

Fulfillment

This state indicates "awareness to the cause," and it is the second-highest of the realms. This level signals a higher level of independence. People become conscious of the more significant questions the world poses, and they understand the "why" of things. The law of cause and effect becomes a clear concept. They understand that every cause has an effect, and the universe is always in motion. This concept allows the practitioner to fully understand that every thought, intention, action, and emotion they experience will have a ripple effect on the universe.

The Divine omniscient will work with them to observe fully and use effort and meditation to become a better person. When meditating, they will use their altered state to be present and mindful of their actions in the physical world.

Learning

The alternate name for this state is "hearing the voice," and it corresponds to people interested in deeper levels of knowledge. They will use their senses to guide them to the truth and learn how to block out the external stimuli that can be misguiding. This process is known as interception and is the ability to look beyond the five senses and recognize what your body and mind are telling you. Practitioners become more aware of how the body and mind are connected. This level of understanding is often accompanied by an elevated health regimen as the understanding of subtle warnings from the body are recognized.

Ecstasy

The first of the inferior levels is the state of being happy because of outside influences. This differs from being enlightened and feeling at peace because it is a temporary state subject to change. This state may feel euphoric, and the interpreter may feel like they are a celestial being, but it can all change in a noticeably short time.

Humanity

People who reach this state are in a controlled state of mind. They learn of higher levels of morality and recognize with clarity the difference between right and wrong. They feel in control and responsible for their destiny so they can take chances and show their vulnerability in the face of negativity. This stage of mind is a chance to advance to a superior state.

Rage

Also called the state of upset. People in this state are prone to negative characteristics. They compare themselves to others and act according to their assumptions. They become overbearing and superior with people they view as lesser beings while becoming subservient and fawning with people they believe to be their betters. There is a tendency to compare yourself with others and dedicate your every thought to changing. Selfish goals overtake your thoughts and can lead to actions that are less than noble. If someone stays in this state too long, it can lead to serious problems with self-esteem.

Animality

When people reach this state, they retreat to their base instincts. Animals fear those who are strong and relish bullying the weak. They rely on their instincts and spend their time fighting to exist without finding the time to be creative. This base state of mind is characterized by foolishness and impulsiveness. If someone stays in the realm of animality, they will evolve their feelings of loyalty and generosity.

Hunger

Also known as the Buddhist state of hungry ghosts, this is the realm of insatiable desires. People residing in this state will be powered by the relentless pursuit of material possessions. There are demons and spirits in this realm that can be harmful to humans, and they can also manifest as paranormal encounters. People in this realm will be eaten up by the desire to become wealthy or famous, and their sleeping hours can be plagued by disturbing images like dark forests, endless staircases, and the feeling of abandonment.

Hell

Also known as the world of suffering. The first teaching of Buddha is that we all need to experience suffering, and those who refuse to acknowledge pain and depression are delusional. This realm is a steppingstone for other realms and must be experienced before true enlightenment can be experienced. Most successful people have a history of suffering and difficulty they transcend before achieving success.

People who emerge from this realm of Buddhism will inevitably be fortified by their experiences. They refuse to allow external forces to influence their true paths and will use their inbuilt resilience to create valuable role models for others.

These ten realms are in no particular order, and Buddhists will experience them in different ways. Interpreting the realms will differ between branches of the religion and be affected by individual teachers. They differ from Judaism as they represent more negative aspects of life.

Buddhism may be the religion you first think about when the term reincarnation is mentioned, but the idea that the soul is transported from human to animal form is not part of the teachings. Buddhism liberates its followers from more traditional practices of religion. It focuses on the fusion of the imaginary world with reality to elevate the mind. It doesn't focus on the soul and believes that the mental construct known as "the self" is the ruling force behind our existence.

The Christian Perspective on Reincarnation

Most people believe that reincarnation has no part to play in Christian teachings, but some Bible sources suggest this wasn't always so. The Hebrew scriptures and early teachings contain references to rebirth that suggest it was commonly accepted that your soul would visit Earth more than once.

This belief may have been discouraged in medieval times as the Roman Church concluded that if people believed they would return to Earth often, they would be less likely to give their wealth to the church. They also decreed that celibacy for priests was necessary to claim the belongings of their ordained brethren.

The Crusades were also a major turning point for Christianity. The church was asking its members to donate all their worldly goods to those that fought in the name of Jesus, so

they needed a system that rewarded and punished their followers. The concept of Heaven and Hell was born. Those that donated went to Heaven to live with God and the angels, while those who refused to donate would spend eternity roasting in the fiery pits of Hell. Reincarnation would have diluted the belief in eternal joy or misery, so the Christian church dispelled any notion of rebirth and a chance to atone for wrongdoings.

Chapter 3: The Wiccan Perspective

Wicca is used to describe a system of beliefs that spans a spectrum of pagan religions and beliefs. It has been around for longer than any other popular religion and is claimed to have been evident as long as thirty-five thousand years ago. While some experts claim that shamanism, as practiced by Native Americans, is the most ancient form of worship, Wicca is spiritually descended from the same rites and can be classed as shamanic.

Ancient Wicca may have been around for centuries, but the modern form of the religion is less than one hundred years. In the 1940s, a man named Gerald Gardner reignited interest in the ancient crafts and wrote a series of books on witchcraft and the origins of Wicca. He described his initiation into a coven of witches in England and his first encounter with the term Wicca.

He explained that the term had a profound effect on him, and he described his link with the "Old Religion" and the oath of silence he had to take. In the 1950s, he founded a branch of the religion known as Gardnerian Wicca following the repealing of England's laws that made witchcraft illegal. His Book of Shadows became a staple part of modern Wiccan beliefs, and the spells, rituals, and lore within it were heavily influenced by Gardner's belief in reincarnation.

Raymond Buckland met Gerald Gardner in 1963, a year before his death, and became the ambassador of Wicca in the United States. He became a leading light in promoting the religion and wrote prolifically on the subject. He was dubbed the "Father of American Wicca" in 1966, and the Museum of Witchcraft and Magick was created in his name in New York. The collection and the museum have been reborn in several destinations and is currently being restored in Ohio as the Buckland Museum.

The appeal of Wicca is the fluidity of its beliefs. It embraces different gods and goddesses and bases its worship depending on individual needs. The modern world is focused on being "green" and saving the planet, so the neopagan nature of Wicca is particularly appealing to eco-warriors. Wiccans s believe the Earth is a living deity that must be cared for and treated like the Goddess in everything. They believe that we must live in harmony with nature and treat the Earth with respect.

Because Wicca has strong female spiritual ties, it appeals to women who want to escape from the patriarchal constructs of more formal religions. Wicca offers them a way to celebrate the goddess that lies within while retaining their feminine essence.

Wicca doesn't believe in setting rules or directions for its followers. It believes that individuality and magic will help its followers choose the path that suits them and their needs. Followers can practice as a solitary witch or join a coven of people with similar beliefs. There are at least 15 types of Wiccan witches and practitioners to choose from, some of the most popular depending on their interests and skills.

Types of Wiccan Witches

- **Eclectic Witches:** These witches don't follow traditional practices or religions. They prefer to follow their own path and turn to their "higher self" to derive their own studies and practices.

- **Faery Witch:** Like the eclectic witch, they believe their doctrine works best for themselves. The difference is they will often seek communication with the faery folk to help them craft their ceremonies.

- **Hedge Witch:** Often, powerful healers or midwives hedge witches can communicate with the spirit world. The word hedge is used to signify the barrier between the two realms, and a hedge witch will often specialize in crossing the boundary to deliver important missives from the spirits.

- **Kitchen Witch:** Despite the name, a kitchen witch is not confined to the traditional idea of a room in which she will cook. Instead, she will make her home and surroundings into a magical place where she can perform her ceremonies and rituals. She uses traditional plants and herbs to produce potions and spells that will enhance the lives of those who seek her help.

- **Dianic Witch:** This is the most feminine form of witchcraft and focuses primarily on the goddess Diana. Her three aspects, the maiden, the mother, and the crone, are all worshiped as Dianic witches reach their age-related goal posts. Unlike the other types of witches, Dianic Wicca is always practiced by females. There was a branch in the 1950s named Arcadian witchcraft that originated halfway through the 20th century, designed to give men the same status as these divine women.

- **Augury Witch:** These witches are primarily involved in deciphering ancient signs and symbols that will indicate if travelers are on the right path to spirituality.

- **Ceremonial Witch:** As the name suggests, these witches practice rituals and ceremonies to hone their craft. They believe in the power of ritual and will often use more modern techniques to improve their understanding of the power they can attract. Some witches will study sacred mathematics or metaphysical beliefs to improve their knowledge of their Wiccan rites.

This list is just a few of the Wiccan witch examples, and if followers want to define themselves in another way, they are encouraged to do so. Wicca is a fluid form of worship, and this influences how they deal with the subject of reincarnation.

Too many religions are caught up with answering the question "What happens when you die?" and dictate what their followers believe. Many proclaim to have the answer, but surely no single explanation is currently available covering everybody's concerns. Wicca believes it may have some answers, but it doesn't believe in setting down doctrines. Some people within Wicca believe in the afterlife, and some don't.

What do Wiccans believe about reincarnation?

This is perhaps the most widely believed concept among practitioners, as being reborn is finely attuned with nature. Most natural processes are cyclical, from the smallest nucleon to the largest planet in the solar system. We all rely on a recurrent system to maintain natural life forms. Wiccan believers have different ideas of how reincarnation works.

Some believe that we begin our journey as the lowliest creatures and transmigrate through a spiritual pecking order until we reach the human form. They believe the soul grows and learns as it passes through a cycle of rebirth. Some believers believe that we are only reincarnated as humans and that the natural world has a different form of reincarnation. This form of belief can also be applied to extra-terrestrial lives if the practitioner believes in life on other planets.

Some people see the journey as a progressive one that has predestined levels of ascension, while others have different beliefs. They believe that the soul chooses the path it wants to take in the next life and defines the form it wants to return to. Others believe in the wheel of fate idea. A random decision defines the whole process, and we get whatever comes, no matter what we have done in previous lives. Some people believe that the form we are reincarnated as depends solely on the karma we created in our former lives.

Whatever they believe is the driving force behind the fate we can expect most Wiccans believe there is a place beyond death where spirits go to rest and recuperate before they return to Earth. This place is called the "Land of Youth" or, more commonly, Summerland. Pagans are generally dismissive of the concept of the afterlife. They know there is a cycle of lives that form the cycle of existence, but they have very few beliefs that embrace the period between these cycles. Wiccans believe there is a need to rest between lives, and they understand the tripartite nature of the soul and why it needs to regenerate.

Wiccans believe that in our incarnate life, the human body, the spirit, and the soul are all co-joined, and when we die, they separate and need to rest. In Summerland, there is the opportunity for the spirit to rest and rejuvenate. The soul is destined to rejoin the Original Source and await reincarnation while the physical body is left behind on Earth. The spirit needs to recover from the attachments it has formed with its previous life and gain a different perspective.

Summerland allows the spirit to meet with others and interact with them. It will remain attached to spirits it has formed attachments within the last life, but it needs a vacation. It will have the opportunity to seek guidance from the ancestors who dwell there and connect with earthbound witches from beyond the veil that separates the two realms.

Summerland is often compared to the Christian concept of Heaven, but this is a common misconception. Others believe it is a place like Valhalla in the Norse religion, which is also inaccurate. Summerland is the place you need it to be to recover from the strains that have been placed on your spirit. Think of an oasis that takes the form you feel most comfortable with, and that is your personal Summerland. You create your own reality here, and you can be with whomever you feel like hanging out with.

If you still have trouble picturing what this looks like, try popular media for a source of reference. Nexus was a place visited by Starfleet in 2293 in the film Star Trek: Generations when members of Starship Enterprise discovered the doorway to the phenomenon. When asked what it was like, they described a sensation of being "pure inside joy as if it was tangible, like a blanket." They described a place in which every desire or thought was the defining source of reality. Time and space were irrelevant, and the peace they felt there was overwhelming.

This is how most Wiccans picture Summerland. There is no pain or suffering, just a place to rest. Some believe this is the plane on which you can choose your next incarnation and review your former existence.

The author A.J. Crew has expanded the theory behind Summerland and laid out a case for Winterland as a place of retribution and punishment. In his book, "A Wiccan Bible," he argues that the theory of Winterland is firmly rooted in Pagan beliefs based on the lore of a Hell-like place where souls who had accumulated karmic debts were sent to atone. Although the term Hell originated in Pagan lore, most Wiccans question the purpose of such a place. They believe that karma will follow in future lives and repay any misdeeds the soul has accumulated.

What if there was a case for Winterland? Consider the case of a witch who has grossly misused their powers and caused great harm to others. Is it enough to send them back to Earth without a time for reflection? Winterland, or the concept of it, offers such souls a place to go to reflect on their deeds before they travel to Summerland to enjoy the rest and peace it promises. Could there be a place of contemplation where souls can search for answers and adjust their attitude to the powers they hold, or is it just a myth?

Wiccans will tell you that if you believe Winterland exists and you live your life accordingly, then that's fine. They believe we all may form our own opinions on death, the afterlife, and reincarnation.

Free Spirits

Some Wiccans believe that their souls are freed from their bodies when they die and make their own choices about what happens next. They can become part of the reincarnation cycle of existence, or they can explore the vast expanses of time and space free from restraints. Imagine traveling between history and the future in just the blink of an eye. Transport yourself back to Roman times to witness the Empire's emergence or blink yourself forward when man resides on Mars. The options are endless. You could choose to watch your family and their descendants through generations, or you could just go to sleep and rest eternally. This is the true meaning of becoming a free spirit.

One idea that can encompass different ideas is that unworthy spirits are not banished to Winterland; instead, they remain trapped on Earth. They could roam the Earth until the Gods and Goddesses feel they have atoned for their negativity or misdeeds in their last life. Some Wiccans believe that people who have died unexpectedly or have issues they need to resolve can be bound to Earth for some time. They will then become ghosts or spirits who haunt the places with which they are associated. Sometimes these spirits can be threatening and take the form of poltergeists or other irreverent spirits.

Not all branches of Wicca believe in reincarnation in its more traditional form. They look to nature for their beliefs, and they see the cycles of life differently. They recognize that seeds and plants produce fruit and flowers every season, but they argue that every growth is individual. This would be like the dead leaves and flowers that decay and are absorbed into the ground and then contribute to the life energy of the universe.

These Wiccans believe that the human body fills the same purpose. The warm ashes or the physical corpse serve as food for the Earth. To quote the biblical text Genesis 3:19, "Ashes to ashes, dust to dust." Life after death simply doesn't play a part in their beliefs, and they believe that once the lights go out, that's it, and our time on Earth is done.

Finally, what happens when our cycle of reincarnation ends? After we have passed through the different existences we are destined to experience, what happens to our souls? Again, Wiccans look to nature for inspiration, and they have a popular chant that sings about what happens when the final time for rest occurs.

"Everyone comes from the Goddess, and everyone will eventually return to her, like a drop of rain returns to the sea."

The Divine source is fueled by the souls of humans who have reached the zenith of their journey. When we are fulfilled and have reached our best self, we join the Goddess to become at one with her forever.

Overall, Wiccans aren't overly concerned with death and the afterlife. They prefer to live in the moment and make sure every second they spend alive is filled with wonder. They believe that all Earthly elements have a soul and that when we die, destiny will take care of our essence and place it where it needs to be. This may be in the air we breathe, the trees that fill the forests, or the water or animals.

As humans, there is bound to be curious about what happens when we die, and that's only normal. Wiccans don't fear death. They embrace it as the natural end to life. Saying goodbye to those who have passed away is a spiritual ritual, and they believe in honoring their dead.

A Guide for How to Honor the Dead Wiccan Style

If your loved one passed away some time ago, you might want to perform these rituals at Samhain, which is October 31st, or the day of the dead, November 2nd, when the veil between the two realms is thinnest. If you feel pain and distress at someone's recent passing, then these services may bring you peace.

Private Ritual

Create an altar dedicated to your loved one. This can be a traditional altar or a part of your home – like a windowsill or tabletop. Cover the surface with a white cloth and place a picture of them on top. You can put a dish of food or a beverage they loved alongside the picture and place a candle or a light beside them. If you both shared a love of nature, put a small bunch of flowers on the altar. You get the picture. Make it personal to the two of you.

Now, cast a circle with a cleansing agent like lavender or sage and light the candle. Invite your loved ones to join you in the circle and offer them your gifts. Once you feel their presence, *just talk to them.* Tell them you miss them and how much you love them. Listen while they talk to you and let them speak freely. Once the time has passed, release them from this life and wish them well. You can tell them that your bond will never break, and they will always be with you in life and death.

Public Ceremony

Sharing your grief with others can be an immensely powerful experience. If you feel like this is a ritual you would like to share with your friends, it need not be overly Pagan or Wiccan-based. This is a memorial service that all denominations can attend.

The Basic Structure of a Public Memorial

• Set up a memorial like an altar described above. Ask everybody to contribute something to it.

• Let everybody take a moment to compose themselves and enjoy a quiet minute before the memorial begins.

• A song you all love or a passage from poetry can help focus the room.

• As the lead celebrant, state your belief that your loved one is in the room and is ready to hear every person within.

• Now let everybody speak if they are comfortable doing so. Encourage stories about your loved ones, both happy and sad. Ask if anyone has anything they would say to the person if they were physically in the room. There are no rules to follow; this memorial is a healing process and can take any form you are all happy with.

• Reaffirm your belief that everyone has been heard and you have all strengthened your bonds of love. Say goodbye and snuff the candle as you end the memorial. Another song may feel right and ends proceedings on a light note.

Chapter 4: Good Karma, Bad Karma

Karma describes how the actions of our former life influence the experiences we will face in our future lives. In Buddhist scriptures, there is a prophecy that in the future, a man will be born called Maitreya, who will have achieved the state of complete enlightenment and teach the doctrine of Dharma to the unenlightened people of the Earth.

He will appear with a soul that has reached the next level of spirituality currently experienced by the Buddha and known as a Bodhisattva. In Sanskrit, this means "enlightened being," and he will be the savior of humankind. In theory, we can all achieve this status and be reborn as a Bodhisattva but, until that time, we need to learn how we are affected by karma and how we can heal in this life.

Some people feel like karma is the bad guy who is the reason behind everything bad that happens to us. We also feel like bad karma is the payback for those who have done us harm. Lives can be spent chasing karmic debts and feeling sorry for yourself with no healing taking part.

You can avoid these common pitfalls by understanding these pertinent facts about karma:

1) Karma is Unbiased and Neutral: The universe has a plan for all of us, and this involves soul contracts in which we pledge to lead the best lives possible. Fearing karma can hold you back from leading a worthy life as you will always wonder what the comeback will be for every action you take. Remember, we are all equal in the eyes of the Divine Source, so you will get what you deserve, no more, no less.

2) Deal with Your Karmic Debt with Style: If you find yourself faced with huge problems and troubles in life, what do you do? Do you request the higher being to give you a break or start seeing your troubles' positive elements? The bigger the issues you must deal with, the more karmic debt you are clearing.

3) You Will Have to Deal with Karma. Nobody can clear your debt to the universe but you. If you try to use spiritual cleansers or spells to deal with your karma, it may delay your experiences, but they will be rerouted back in the future.

4) You Aren't a Victim of Karma: Dwelling on the past and the future can distract you from the present. Concentrate on living a good life with honest and truthful intentions, and you will be creating a healthy karmic future while clearing your karmic debt simultaneously.

5) Don't Seek Revenge: The people we encounter may have karmic relationships with you in a former life. This means they have a debt to clear, or they may be creating bad karma for their future. Whatever the case, you need to accept the reasons for their relationship with you. We all have soul contracts to follow, so let them get on with it, and don't try to get your own back. Revenge has no purpose, and you could create your own karmic debt.

This doesn't mean you shouldn't fight your corner, far from it. Get away from toxic relationships and experiences and clear your plate. Don't wait around for karma to hit back, you know it will, but you don't have to witness it. Steer clear of those who bring out the worst in you and seek healthier relationships.

6) Big Karma Means Big Steps: The law of karma is a system that loves to work with you. Don't fear it. Embrace it! Take those big steps and begin to reap the rewards.

The laws of karma can be explained simply, but they are encompassing. The main concept is biblical in its statement. You reap what you sow. The world of science can provide an alternate meaning as karma is the spiritual parallel of the law of motion. For every action, there is an opposite reaction.

Everything in the universe is connected, and if you can only see negative traits and personalities in others, then the problem lies with you. Be a better person and recognize that humans are flawed, but they also have greatness within. We are mirrors to what surrounds us, and if you are focused on negativity, then you are wasting your life.

Live in the here and now and fill yourself with positivity, and you will forget to get angry or feel rage. This is the law of focus that teaches us to concentrate on higher planes of thought rather than base emotions. Karma is an educational tool that should inspire you to live a valuable loving life that contributes to the universe and all who live in it.

What are Karmic Relationships?

These types of relationships will often be the basis for some of our most damaging karmic wounds. They will be formed with souls who differ greatly from yourself, and they will mean conflict. These relationships will often be brief yet intense. They are formed so you can learn a lesson or teach one.

Here are the signs you are in a karmic relationship:

It's Addictive

Normal relationships thrive when the couple have differing interests and enjoy spending time apart. When you are so enthralled with your relationship that you cannot bear to leave their side, this is not healthy. If you feel addicted to them, your psyche knows this isn't good for you, but you can't resist them. If you keep repeating your relationship lows, then it's time to break the addiction.

Consider the Highs and Lows

Normal relationships involve arguments and times of disagreement. People also experience intense joy, and that's okay. When the low periods outweigh or equal the highs, it's time to reevaluate your relationship. If you feel your partner brings out the worst in you, then it's time to let go.

There is No Middle Ground

Normal relationships aren't filled with drama; they wouldn't be healthy if they were. Karmic relationships are like riding a rollercoaster. One day you may be passionately in love, whispering sweet nothings and filled with joy. The next day you are screaming at each other about who left a towel on the bathroom floor. You may not realize that you are that couple who make their friends perform an eye roll when they disagree. If you hear the phrase "Here they go again" or "Drama king and queen," then it may be time to look at how your relationship is developing.

You Defend Them to Your Friends

Even though you know what people say about your partner is true, you can't admit it to anyone, even yourself. You have placed them on a pedestal, and nobody can knock them off. They may drive you crazy, and you know exactly what their faults are saying it out loud kills you. Their flaws define them, and you can't see past that. Your friends are right, but you would rather fall out with them than bad-mouth your partner.

Your Partner is Selfish

Do you constantly find yourself putting them first and forgetting your own identity or needs? You think you are showing your love, but you can become a doormat for them to wipe their feet on. They know you can't live without them, so they wring your emotions and manipulate you.

Healthy relationships involve some give and take. Both partners care about the feelings of the people they love, and they will work as a team. Karmic partners will use your love to get their way.

They are Controlling

They are just as involved in you as you are in them. They need to know where you are and what you're always doing. They need to know you are the center of their universe, just like you consider them to be the center of yours. They are worried you will find other people more interesting than them if you stray too far. If your partner tries to cut your ties to other people, this is a classic sign you are in a karmic relationship.

The bottom line is we all need karmic relationships to teach us important facts about love and life. They are essential for self-growth, providing you deal with them correctly. Once you recognize the toxicity within your relationship, you need to cut them out of your life, no matter how hard that is. They have an emotional pull for you that can be hard to ignore. Stay strong and know that you have learned from the relationship, and maybe they have too.

How to Generate Good Karma

Wayne Dyer, the motivational speaker and self-help guru, made an exceptionally good point when he said, "How people treat you is their karma. How you react is your karma." You can't stop people from doing negative actions, but you can react with positivity.

Most people live their lives on autopilot and aren't aware of their impact on others. A throwaway comment or negative energy can have huge repercussions for the people you meet. Much of the strife in the world today results directly from people's thoughts. Social media is filled with anger and negativity, and all the bickering, complaining, and unhappiness cannot fail to cause sorrow to those it is aimed at.

When was the last time you felt positive after checking your Twitter feed? Can you feel the negative energy that has engulfed the whole planet recently? Nobody says that posting a nasty comment on social media is the root cause but think of what would happen if we were all more conscious of our impact on others?

We need to counter this collective negative energy and raise the vibrational levels of positivity. You can do your bit by remembering to apply these tips to raise your karma:

Tell the Truth

"Every time you tell a lie, a fairy dies" is a popular English saying that parents use to encourage their children to always tell the truth. While most adults don't believe in fairies, the sentiment remains true! If you are caught out in a lie, you make yourself look untrustworthy and deceitful. Other people won't trust you, and your reputation will be damaged.

Telling the truth allows people with the same moral compass to enter your life. You will feel better knowing that your circle of friends and colleagues is a trustworthy group living authentically. Lying drains your energy as you need to monitor your deceits and remember details of falsehoods. Telling the truth is better for your health and generally more positive.

Offer Compliments

When you compliment someone, sincerely it can change their lives. It may encourage their self-esteem and help them achieve greatness, or it may just make their day. If you find it difficult to give a compliment, start with small gestures. Tell your partner they look good or tell a colleague they are good at their job. Once you experience the positivity a compliment will bring, it is easier to give them more freely.

Help People in Need

Having a purpose in life can mean you become a little self-centered. Being ambitious and driven is not a bad thing, but you need to make time for others. Volunteer for charity work or community projects in your free time and give something back. Helping people you know can also be satisfying, and there will always be someone who will appreciate your unique talents and traits.

When you feel empty or lost, offer your help to someone, and you will feel better. Good deeds and kind actions will help you fill any void in your life that may be causing you to feel low.

Work

Unemployment will sometimes happen. That is a fact of life but how you deal with it is not. If you mope around at home waiting for your next unemployment check, then you are bound to feel negative about your situation. Get off your butt and do something about it. Volunteer for local causes, take on an internship, or simply turn up where you would like to work. Enthusiasm for work is a key part of life, and it gets your positive juices going.

Take on a part-time position but put in full-time hours. Pitch in whenever you can, and it will help you progress in life. Fulfilling work is everybody's dream, but we all must start somewhere. Even the most mundane position offers opportunities for enthusiasm and energy. Fill your days with activity, and you will sleep better and feel healthier.

Give Someone Else a Chance

If you are lucky enough to have a good job or a position of importance, then great, but it can still be a worrying time for everyone at the moment. Financial insecurity is a key part of modern life, but sometimes you must think of others. Stop worrying about how long you will have a job and make things better for someone else. Make a connection or recommendation to help someone else's career prospects improve, and your karma will grow.

Say Thank You Regularly

Most successful people realize the importance of the people who work with them. The guys who keep the wheels turning while they are the driving force. The difference between people who are respected and those who are loved by their workforce can often be a simple thank you. Respected and successful people can climb the career ladder and top their field, but earning love from others takes an extra ounce of effort.

John F. Kennedy famously said, "We must find time to stop and thank the people who make a difference in our lives." Saying thank you costs nothing yet gives plenty. From the guy who parks your car to the cashier at the supermarket, give them a sincere "thank you" for their effort. Most people appreciate even the simplest form of appreciation for what they do.

Live Purposefully

Whatever you do with your life, make sure it's filled with clear intentions. Set goals for yourself, and you will attract like-minded people. The universe will send energy-filled experiences and people to make your journey more fulfilling.

Give Away Something Valuable

This can be a material gift or something less physical. Giving possessions and effects can be immensely satisfying, but so can give someone your resources. For instance, if you are a writer offered a job that isn't a good fit for you, consider other people in your field. Do you know another writer who may be perfect for this project? Being selfless and generous will score high on your karma scoresheet.

Become a Mentor

Sharing your skills is a perfect way to give something back. Most successful people will have experienced some form of mentorship, and great leaders understand that they can fulfill this role for others. Sometimes the transition from an individual performer into a leader can take time. Stick with it. Sharing knowledge is a mighty gift to give.

Show Kindness

Some people believe kindness and a forgiving nature is a sign of weakness. They are signs of strength when it comes to karma. Nobody goes through life without hurting or being hurt by someone else. The hard part can be getting over it and moving on. True believers in karma will recognize that bad experiences or hurtful people are signs of past karma coming to bite them on the butt. To spread good karma, stop all your harmful ways and forgive those who have given you bad vibes in the past.

Show Up

One of the most overlooked ways of spreading good karma is also one of the simplest. Being there for people can be incredibly powerful. When your friend has an important day ahead, ask them if they need support. Just knowing you're prepared to be there for them will give them a boost.

Always keep your word and turn up to events you have promised to attend. It doesn't matter if the weather is awful or getting to the event is difficult. You need to put in the effort whenever possible. When people make an effort and aren't rewarded with interest, it can stop them from trying again. Be the cheerleader for your friends and always turn up.

Chapter 5: Discover Your Soul Type

Your soul is the innermost essence of your higher self. Just like your body is filled with millions of cells, there are only a few different types of cells. Just like there are millions of souls in the universe, there are only seven types of souls.

The best way to describe it is to imagine the Highest Being, the Original Source, or God; whatever your belief is, we all recognize the need for an absolute source of energy, standing alone before a glass prism. As the light and energy from the source pass through the prism, it casts a rainbow of colors that reflect the seven soul types. Each of these types has a role in fulfilling the greater scheme of things. There are no forms of ranking within the soul types, and they all have a role to play.

The nature of the roles assigned to soul types:

- Whatever your soul type, the role you play will come naturally. Nothing is forced or imposed on anyone; they are just who they are.

- The archetypal names the soul types have are far from politically correct, and they do not influence the roles we play in life. King souls don't automatically hold "higher positions" than Server souls.

- Despite the name, there is no gender assignment involved. Souls have no gender and will choose between the roles to fit the life they are about to live. The present queen of England, Elizabeth the second, is the longest-reigning monarch yet has a Server soul.

- Children will often show their true soul identity, but as adolescents, they will begin to mask their traits due to social programming, egoistic reasons, or cultural pressure. When they reach mid-life, a true soul character may cast aside the shackles that have governed their early life and show their true calling. For example, a female Warrior who has spent her early life raising a family may run for political office. A male Artisan who spent his twenties rising through the business world ranks may give it up and become an organic farmer who paints.

- Your soul type is permanent, but everything else can change. A Warrior soul can be incarnated as a policeman first, a housewife next, then a child prodigy and an actress, and so life goes on. Whatever their human lives contain, their soul will be the same. They will be great communicators who love to surround themselves with people. They will be well-spoken and knowledgeable no matter what their social standing is.

What are the seven types, and what are their roles?

1: The Server Soul

They are nature's caretakers who seek to make the world a better place for everyone. They are often modest and unassuming, yet they strive to help people on all levels. They care about their families and can be disappointed when they fail to live up to certain standards. The truth is they have the woes of the world on their shoulders, and they are often considered harmless looking.

Server souls are often found in medical careers, public service roles like policemen, ambulance, and social work, and they can also succeed in politics. They comprise 30% of the population.

What Do Server Souls Look Like?

They are gentle souls, and this is reflected in their faces. Their heads are round and shaped like a potato with soft, undefined features. They can look weary and downtrodden, and their shoulders will typically sag and give them a rounded shape.

Famous Server Souls

Queen Elizabeth the second. She has strong family ties and thinks of her subjects as extensions of that family. She is in her 90s and shows no sign of slowing down or quitting her duties.

Desmond Tutu: The South African cleric is known for his tireless work to promote human rights and conquer anti-apartheid struggles. He has faced immense struggles during his life, yet he continued to fight for activist causes throughout his life. He is retired but continues to be a leading light in the battle for racial equality.

Florence Nightingale: Known as the Lady of the Lamp, she was a prominent social reformer who came to prominence during the Crimean War. Considered the founder of modern medicine, she highlighted the need for reform in the Victorian era.

The Dalai Lama is the 14th holder of the spiritual title given by the Tibetan people to their chosen leader and is Tenzin Gyatso. He is a Server soul currently using his words of wisdom to create calming a panic-stricken world dealing with a deadly pandemic. He is committed to the cultivation of warmth and kindness in a world that is hurting.

2: The Artisan Soul

These souls take their creative thoughts and transform them into reality. They embrace creativity and believe in originality. They thrive on creating things, and anything counts for quenching their thirst for individuality. Artisan souls work well in all industries that involve creation. This can be as diverse as a scientific theorem or a piece of poetry.

Think of all the cool stuff in the world: apps that control your home, engineers who have designed the fastest cars on the road, or architects who have constructed amazing buildings. They form around 22% of the population and will work in trades that reflect their skills. They can often come across as ditzy and fanciful because their thoughts are filled with creative ideas, and they tend to be deep in thought.

What Do Artisan Souls Look Like?

They have heart-shaped faces with composed and even features. They will often look like they are sitting for a portrait while looking dreamily into the heavens. Their eyes will appear dreamy and filled with soft lights that suggest their hidden depths. They will often show glee and delight in a childlike manner, and their playfulness will be evident.

Famous Artisan Souls

Elvis Presley: Regarded as one of the most significant cultural icons of the 20th century, Elvis was a flamboyant personality who lived for his music. His style appealed to the masses, and he progressed into films and television with ease. He has inspired generations of musicians, from Jerry Lee Lewis to Prince, and his general air of humility combined with talent continues to leave a legacy of musical importance even today.

Steven Spielberg: One of the most influential personalities in the history of films, Spielberg has influenced the cinematic industry like no other individual. He discovered his passion early in life, and he became one of the youngest TV directors in the late 1960s. His film repertoire is filled with a diverse list of productions that range from the childlike wonder that inspired ET to the historical dramas like Schindler's List. His imaginative fantasy films are filled with traditional action and fictional monsters that have been the stuff of dreams for children for decades.

Jamie Oliver: This British chef is one of the most enthusiastic people in the industry. His passion for food is infectious, and he has published numerous books on the subject. Besides J. K. Rowling, he is the most published person on the planet.

3: Warrior Souls

As the name suggests, they are active types who love competition. Challenges are there to test the warrior spirit, and these souls believe they are the road to success. Hard work attracts them like a magnet, and they will be physically strong and ready to go to battle. They will often be soft-spoken yet forceful, and they will be loyal to the end. They can be blunt and feisty, leading others to find them rude.

Warriors cause 17% of the population and are the athletes, soldiers, and top-earning salesmen.

What Do Warrior Souls Look Like?

They have jar-shaped heads with a strong jawline. Warrior souls will have solid bodies that are firm-skinned and accustomed to the outdoors. Their overall persona is hard and angular, and their expression is often combatant. Expressively they are ready for anything and can look vicious and ruthless.

Famous Warrior Souls

Mike Tyson: Known as the "Baddest Man on the Planet," Mike Tyson has a background that could have led him to a life of crime. He was regularly in trouble with the law but turned himself around and became the most successful boxer in the world.

He is also a convicted rapist and was sent to prison for six years for his crimes. Tyson is a typical Warrior soul as he is still battling to return to the sport he loves and mend his reputation. He believes in the mantra that actions speak louder than words and has led his life as a true example of Warrior mentality.

Judi Dench: This formidable British actress can silence a room with just a look. At 87, she is still working and is considered a leading actress in Hollywood. She is a prolific campaigner for charities and has raised money for dementia and the theatre industry. Dame Judi has played roles in children's classics like Angelina Ballerina and The Chronicles of Narnia while also appearing in gritty dramas like Iris and Tea with Mussolini.

4: Scholar Souls

Born with a natural ability to seek and retain knowledge, these souls will always excel in academia. They rarely express their emotions in public and can be considered cold fish. Some people will find them arrogant and detached, and their nerdiness will often make them loners even though they are easygoing. Scholars love to share their knowledge, but this can make them seem boastful and full of themselves.

Responsible for 13% of the population, they are more comfortable in the fields of research and science. They love to work alone or share their knowledge as teachers and professors.

What Do Scholar Souls Look Like?

Scholars tend to look like intelligent robots with large foreheads. They appear robotic due to the lack of expression and the deadpan features they display. Their attention is generally focused on their thoughts, which can leave them looking detached and uninterested in their surroundings.

Famous Scholar Souls

Marie Curie: The first woman to win a Nobel prize, Curie was the poster girl for women hell-bent on achieving their dream. She began life in poverty and worked hard for five years to gain entrance to the famed Sorbonne. She formed a relationship with an equally brilliant man, Pierre Curie, and they married in 1895. The scientific-devoted duo discovered polonium and radium, which led to major medical breakthroughs.

Emma Thompson: Dame Emma Thompson was born into a family of actors, yet she had an academic background. She attended Cambridge University and was a popular student known for her wit and intelligence. Her relationships with the members of the popular Footlights Group would lead to a successful career in entertainment. She is a fearless character who has no illusions about her shortcomings and is known for her self-satire.

5: Sage Souls

They are people who love the limelight. Not always original thinkers, they rely on wit and charm to win over people. Their ability to perform naturally often sees them as the heart and soul of the party, and they thrive on the attention. Sage souls represent 11% of the population and are happy in careers like entertainment, teachers, and public speakers.

What Do Sage Souls Look Like?

Their facial features are open and accessible. Sage souls use their faces to communicate their happiness, so their cheeks are often plump and prominent. They have generous mouths that love to smile, and the overall effect is a face that looks like a balloon.

Famous Sage Souls

Jack Black: The ultimate smiley clown Jack Black loves to entertain people. Every picture you see of him looks happy. If he isn't smiling, his eyes are twinkling and full of mischief. Behind the silly facade, a successful business brain is always working. He recently created a best-selling line of skincare and shaving products that have added to his already high net worth.

Mariah Carey: Some people think this songbird is a diva, and she has been accused of some outlandish behavior. Her staff has a different story to tell. They reported that Mariah is generous and loyal with a kind heart who knows them all by name. Mariah is also known as the "Queen of Christmas," and that is very Sage-like.

6: Priest Souls

These types of souls are compassionate, caring, and spiritual. They nurture humanity and account for 7% of the population. Priest souls are often found in religious roles or social work, or counseling.

What Do Priest Souls Look Like?

They tend to have almond shape heads with cat-like eyes. The Priestly expression can range from stern anger to high enthusiasm depending on their focus. They often have a gaze that is hypnotic and strikingly intense.

Famous Priest Souls

Christopher Walken: This American actor is famed for his piercing gaze and nervous disposition. He has appeared in over 100 films and TV shows and is currently starring in Severance.

Joan of Arc: The Maid of Orleans was born in 1412 in France and was a national heroine of the country. She led the French army to a famous victory over the English. Despite her tender age, she was a great leader acting under divine guidance. Her beliefs led to her death in 1431 when she was burned as a heretic.

7: King Souls

Kings are great at problem-solving and make great leaders. They can be arrogant and sometimes ruthless when people don't match their exacting standards. The King souls account for 13% of the population and can be found in government roles. Political office or as managers and leadership positions where their skills can be utilized.

What Do King Souls Look Like?

They have a distinguished look with a broad face and a hard jawline. Their expression can vary from a look of authority that tells you they know what they are doing to a withering scowl that tells you they know you don't have a clue what you are doing.

Famous King Souls

Simon Cowell: Anybody who has watched Simon Cowell judging talent shows know exactly what his style is. He is the king of the putdown and lets the contestants know what he thinks.

Sarah Palin: This lady doesn't pull punches. She is a typical female King soul, and her opinions match her type.

What kind of soul are you? Take this quiz and discover:

Question 1: There is a bad storm in your area, and you have the day off. What do you do?

　　a) Have a day pampering yourself. You deserve a day of luxury.

b) Spend the day watching documentaries and historical programs on television.

c) Spend the day playing board games with your family.

d) Make sure your neighbors are okay and clear the snow from their drives as they need to go out.

e) Reconnect with your old friends whom you haven't seen for a while. Maybe phone them or write a letter.

f) Have a cook-out as bad weather doesn't worry you in the slightest.

g) Spend the day dancing to your favorite tunes and let your hair down.

Question 2: You are planning a trip to a foreign country, what do you do to prepare?

a) I do nothing. I buy my ticket and just go. That's part of the experience for me.

b) Hire local guides and let them take me to non-touristy places of interest.

c) I talk to everyone I am traveling with and discover what makes them happy, then book it.

d) I find historically significant places and plan my accommodations to fit in with my tour.

e) I choose spiritual places in the area to visit and love to check out architectural sites.

f) I love luxury on holiday and choose the best restaurants and hotels.

g) I choose the liveliest resorts filled with activities and have busy nightlife. Sleep is the last thing on my mind.

Question 3: Choose a motto that sums up your attitude toward life:

a) All the world is a canvas for my work. The drama will occur, but it will sort itself out.

b) When I know what's real and have done my research, I will know my true path.

c) I am an important cog in a much larger machine. I play my part, and I am happy to do so.

d) I am the master of my own destiny, and I may cause casualties on my journey.

e) I have single-minded devotion to a higher goal.

f) Strength guides me, and I am happy to be a role model for others.

g) Love and kindness are essential, and so is fun.

Question 4: You are on a journey to meet a friend, and time is short. You encounter a roadblock, and you can't access Google maps. What do you do?

a) Search maps you have in the car for an alternative route.

b) Check out why the blockage has occurred, and then make your mind up about what you will do.

c) Call your friend and arrange to meet in a place that is more accessible.

d) Move it out of the way and carry on your journey.

e) Drive around the area looking for an alternative route.

f) Check the road is safe and then drive around the blockade.

g) Ask locals for help.

Question 5: What type of voluntary work appeals to you the most?

a) Teaching your native language to students from abroad.

b) Tutoring math or science to local kids.

c) Working at food kitchens or homeless shelters.

d) Working as a representative within a UN initiative.

e) Helping at your local church or other religious places.

f) Working for a political campaign.

g) Organizing outdoor activities like camping or hiking for kids from impoverished backgrounds.

Results

If you answered

Mostly a)'s: You are an Artisan soul. You have a lighter look at life and can be creative and playful.

Mostly b)'s: You are a Scholar soul. You are analytical, curious, and naturally seek a neutral path to knowledge.

Mostly c)'s: You are a Server soul. You are nurturing and caring to others. You love to share with others and rarely think of yourself first.

Mostly d)'s: You are a Warrior soul. You have a naturally forceful manner and are protective of others. You are determined and refuse to be daunted by obstacles.

Mostly e)'s: You are a Priest soul. You are a visionary who loves to energize others and seek to be an inspiration to others.

Mostly f)'s: You are a King soul. You are decisive and willing to take control when others cannot. You are a natural leader.

Mostly g)'s: You are a Sage soul: You are entertaining and love to be around other people. You are confident in all social scenarios.

Chapter 6: Are You an Old Soul?

When the subject of reincarnation and aging souls is under discussion, the name *Michael* will often be mentioned. This is because a group of spiritual-seeking individuals formed in the early 1970s to contact some form of higher being via a Ouija board. In 1973, they made contact, and the whole group felt connected to this entity as the board spelled out the message, "We are here with you today."

The group felt they needed to give the entity a name and asked how it would prefer to be known. It replied that the last name the entity had used on Earth was Michael, so the name stuck. The Ouija board then disappeared, and the group used other methods to chat with Michael. Imagine a Cosmic Google that answers every question, in detail and rationally.

Some questions were spiritual, others were personal to the person asking them, and some were generally about life and what happens when we die. This is where the Michael Teachings come to the fore of what happens during the process of reincarnation. The entity taught the group the structure that forms the process and why we need to complete the cycles within to become enlightened beings.

What are the "Michael Teachings"?

According to Michael, there are five steps to evolution, and within each step, seven increments need to be completed. Just like a computer game, you strive to reach higher levels and face greater challenges. This would suggest that humans need to reincarnate 35 (5x7) times to become evolved and learn the lessons needed to achieve spiritual completion.

If only it was that straightforward. As we know from karmic teachings, we don't always get it right in every life we live. Michael tells us that most humans take over 100 lives to reach the state called an old soul. He named the five levels and attached colors to them so we can identify the maturity of the soul in its human form.

What are the five stages known as?

• **Infant Souls**: These less evolved souls will have a pinkish hue to their auras. They are focused on their individual needs and their own survival. They will flourish in small groups or rural settings and are less comfortable in modern society. They lack the social graces that more evolved beings have, and they will often be deemed to have social disorders. While they may be prone to impulsive acts and have little understanding of the consequences they may incur, they are also completely innocent and lack the type of agendas we all adhere to.

• **Baby Souls**: These souls have a darker yellow hue. In contrast to infant souls, Baby souls have a rigid and principled idea of right and wrong. They can appear as conformist and old-fashioned regarding their devout and moralistic ideas about life. Baby souls will often choose to live in highly principled communities that live by a strict set of rules like the Amish or the Old Brethren that ban the use of modern features like electricity. They prefer to adhere to more traditional methods of farming and worship modestly.

- **Young Souls**: Surrounded by a bright yellow aura, these souls are all about the ego. They are fueled by ambition and seek to be famous, successful, wealthy, or all three. Young souls are extroverts and brash. They have their own agenda and no reason to question it. Life for young souls is all about the legacy they leave, as at this stage, most souls are more aware of death yet unsure about reincarnation. This means they are eager to make their mark on society one way or another.

- **Mature Souls**: Basking in their aura's natural green color, mature souls are more open to suggestions. They have abandoned their rigid beliefs and are more inclined to fix their perspectives on how the situation plays out. With relationships, mature souls are less egocentric and focus on the right relationship for them rather than sticking to regular conformities.

At this stage of evolution, mature souls find the need to search for spiritual answers and understand themselves on a deeper level. This can be through art, ideology, or other doctrines that lead to self-growth. Mature souls will also question more. They need to be sure that the beliefs they have are real and based on truth.

- **Old Souls**: Mature souls are bathed in a blue-indigo light and exude a depth of wisdom that radiates from within. When mature souls reach childhood, they will often be described as having an old head on young shoulders. Old souls are happy within their environment and see the world as a stage to observe as they live in their own bubble of knowledge and love. They reject conflict and feel a freedom that can lead to them living a solitary life free from social structures and expectations.

The downside to their wisdom and higher levels of compassion can lead to depression or withdrawal. They find modern life so utterly chaotic and based on superficial goals that they consciously cut ties to modern society and live nomadic lives, constantly seeking new forms of wisdom and spirituality.

There is another level of growth mentioned by the Michael teachings that take place following these Earthly stages. This is called the Elder soul stage and is commonly known as stage six. As this is not strictly a stage of reincarnation, it's important to realize we don't always achieve this level and remain in stage 5.

How do you know you're an old soul?

Do you feel like you've been around for many, many lifetimes? Do people automatically gravitate to you for advice? Consider different civilizations and the importance placed on knowledge and wisdom.

Here are some old souls who have influenced history.

- **Confucius:** He advocated lifelong education, yet it took 2500 years for the concept to enter modern thinking.

- **Charles Dickens:** Regarded as the greatest novelist of the Victorian period, he created literary masterpieces that described Victorian England and the social disparity and poverty common at the time.

- **Erasmus:** A Dutch humanist was critical of the Church, but he kept his faith and produced influential materials that would change the course of religious teachings for the generations that followed. He fought hard for religious tolerance and became a leading light in the reformation of the Catholic Church.

- **Eva Peron:** Known as Evita, she was a powerful force in Argentina in the late 1940s until she died in 1952. She formed the first large-scale female political party and centered her policies on improving the most poverty-stricken citizens' lives and providing free health care.

- **Rosa Parks:** In 1955, Rosa changed the world by refusing to obey a bus drive to vacate her seat so a white passenger could sit down. She became the mother of modern-day civil rights, and her legacy was acknowledged worldwide.

15 Signs that you are an old soul:

1) You have a strong sense of intuition: Deep within the gut, there is a neurotransmitter that signals when danger is present. These feelings trigger the primitive part of the brain that sends us into a state of alert. You automatically know when someone is lying to you or something is "off." This is because learned lessons in your previous lives make you more aware of toxic people.

2) You have a skill for precognition: This is a skill that can be hard to detect even in people with it. If you have an unerring sense of how things will pan out in the future, even before the event has happened, then you have the skill of precognition. Another way to describe the skill is "second sight" or "foretelling the future." It can be seen as a spiritualist skill, and you will be attracted to working with mediums and spiritual healers.

3) Modern trends don't interest you: Popular activities and interests just don't influence you. Traditional pastimes and activities are more appealing, and you will often retreat from the world with a good book or spend time meditating alone.

4) You prefer staying at home with a friend rather than socializing in public places. Loud, noisy bars and restaurants are too raucous for you, and you much prefer quiet places with a traditional atmosphere.

5) People often call you a great source for advice. They tell people you are sage-like and mature beyond your years. You enjoy the comments but don't feel you need to repeat them in a boastful way. If people want to follow your advice, then fine if they don't then that's their decision.

6) You often feel you have a different perspective on life in general. When you need to get an overall view, your consciousness soars, and you look down on the world like an eagle soaring in the sky.

7) Music is a passion for you. You love classical music, but you will try all the genres and appreciate the skill it takes to create all types of music.

8) Time is precious for you even though it may seem like you spend your time dreaming. You consider your contemplative periods as time well spent, and you refuse to rush around experiencing multiple activities. Younger souls are obsessed with packing their time with "new stuff" rather than concentrating on their passions. You will make time for things you love and spend as much time as you like pursuing your passions.

9) When faced with adversity, you always make wise decisions. You are known for being a leader and someone to turn to in times of strife.

10) Generosity is part of your nature. You love giving gifts and witnessing the joy they bring and would rather give a dozen gifts than receive just one.

11) Realism tinged with optimism is how you base your beliefs. You know the world is far from perfect, yet you believe in the intrinsic belief it is good in everyone. You remain forever hopeful there will be good outcomes, yet you know how to cope with negativity.

12) Fashion passes you by. Clothes are merely there to cover your body, and you refuse to conform to modern fashions. You know what suits you and what you feel comfortable in. This doesn't mean you don't have your own sense of style, but that is exactly what it is! Nobody influences you, and you love to wear clothes that reflect your personality.

13) Empathy is a part of your makeup. When someone enters a room, you immediately know what they are feeling. A change in their energy or a shift in your mood will signal a reflection of how they are feeling. Some empaths can pick up on more physical

signs and pain from others and can sense muscular tension or energy blockages.

14) You have unexplained phobias. If you live in the city and have never even visited the beach, why would you have a crippling fear of sharks? What about normal things that are pleasurable to others, yet you feel disgusted whenever you think about them? Flowers, lambs, and puppies are all adorable, yet you feel nothing but nausea when you think about them, signs that your soul has had a bad experience with one or all three.

15) Soul recognition: Old souls refuse to judge people on their actions. They know we are all on a journey, and every action influence that path. You can connect with others on a deeper level and form bonds with many people from all walks of life. Your soul knowledge isn't restricted to humans. Your connections with animals or nature can be just as rewarding or even more so.

Just How Old is Your Soul?

Take this quiz and discover if your soul has been to Earth often or if it is a relative newcomer.

Question 1) How often do you experience déjà vu?

    a) Hardly ever

    b) All the time, I just had it this morning.

    c) Frequently

    d) Occasionally

Question 2) Do you have places that draw you back time after time?

    a) Yes, and I visit them regularly.

    b) No, I love to discover new spots and rarely go back to destinations.

    c) Yes, and I wasn't born there and have *no* family there.

d) Just my childhood hometown

Question 3) Do you feel like you have met people before, even though they are strangers?

a) No, I feel like every time I meet new people, it is a brand-new experience.

b) Not really, but it has probably happened a couple of times.

c) All the time. I have formed some strong connections within minutes of meeting strangers.

d) Sometimes, I feel like I know people even before we have met, and they just feel familiar.

Question 4) How would you describe the style of your home?

a) Always changing, some rooms are modern, and others are more traditional.

b) Midcentury, classic style.

c) Victorian period style

d) I love a bargain, so whatever is on sale, that's what I decorate with.

Question 5) What type of TV program do you prefer?

a) Cowboys and Indians are great. I love Westerns.

b) Period dramas and historical fiction.

c) Sci-fi programs

d) I love classic films in black and white.

Question 6) Do you ever feel like the modern world is going too fast?

a) Not at all. I love technology and can't wait to see regular people travel in space.

b) Yes. I don't own a smartphone or a laptop.

c) Hell yes, I would prefer to live in the woods in an off-grid house and work on my whittling!

d) No, the world is going at a pace we can all keep up with.

Question 7) Did you always know what career or job you would follow when you grew up?

a) Yes, but I did change careers in my mid-twenties.

b) Always I felt a strong connection with my destiny from an early age.

c) No, I always thought I'd figure it out when the time came.

d) I sort of knew but wasn't sure.

Question 8) What age are your main group of friends?

a) Mixed, mostly my own age, but I get along with older people as well.

b) I have friends who are much older than me, and I find people my own age annoying.

c) I love people who are the same age as me or even a couple of years younger.

d) A handful are older than me but mostly my own age.

Question 9) What tradition from the past would you like to see restored?

a) Doing the Charleston while drinking martinis.

b) The tournaments that Knights used to fight in.

c) None. They were abolished for a reason.

d) Village life with maypoles and pagan ceremonies.

Question 10) Do you sometimes hear the voices of people who are no longer with us?

a) not.

b) All the time, and I am comforted by them. They appear when I need help or reassurance.

c) Now and then, but I can tune them out.

d) Quite a lot, doesn't everybody?

How did you score?

1) a) 1 b) 4 c)3 d)2

2) a)4 b) 1 c)3 d)2

3) a)1 b) 2 c) 4 d)3

4) a)3 b) 2 c) 4 d) 1

5) a) 3 b) 4 c) 1 d) 2

6) a)1 b) 3 c) 4 d) 2

7) a) 3 b) 4 c) 1 d) 2

8) a) 2 b) 4 c) 1 d) 3

9) a) 2 b) 3 c) 1 d) 4

10) a) 1 b) 4 c) 2 d) 3

Between 10 and 20

Hello newbie! You are fresh to the world, and while you may have been here before, you are still developing your personality and soul. The world is a fresh and vibrant place for you, and you embrace the future. You are eager to meet new people and form bonds to carry into the spiritual ether, but you aren't sure why. The concept of a spiritual journey is still new to you, and it doesn't impact too much on the life you are currently leading.

Between 20 and 25

You have some age to your soul but are still classed as an infant soul. You view the world with curiosity and wonder, but you have learned important lessons in your former lives.

Between 25 and 30

You are a young soul who has mixed views about the world. Like a human teenager, you understand the modern world is filled with amazing innovations, but you can also recognize the value of retro ideas and historical knowledge.

Between 30 and 35

You are a mature soul who can feel a little jaded with the world as you have been back so often. You are a person filled with wisdom and whom people turn to for advice. You know you have some stuff to learn, but you can see the light at the end of the tunnel as for your spiritual journey.

Between 35 and 40

Hello you! Welcome to the old soul club. You have been there and done that. You can contemplate death with a healthy attitude as you realize that life is short, but death isn't the end. You may feel weary and ready to end your journey through the spiritual realm. You prefer your own company and spend your time seeking those last nuggets of information that may have eluded you before. Other people just interfere with your quest, so you tend to seek solitude.

Chapter 7: Twin Flames and Soulmates

Some people think that both these concepts mean the same thing. They define twin flames and soulmates as the love of their life, the one or your other half. While this is partially true, the two concepts are much more defined and describe different types of relationships.

What are Twin Flames?

Spiritual groups have used the term twin flames for some time but classed them as part of a more generic soul group. Even among spiritual people, the reasoning behind the term was rarely touched upon. In 2014 all that changed. Twin flames and their impact on life seemed to erupt on social media and other popular platforms. Songs were written about the notion of twin flames, and they appeared in Hollywood films. Magazine articles have described the idea behind twin flames, and teens described their toxic first relationships as being the first part of their twin flame journey. Quite simply, the younger generation made Twin Flames glamorous and sexy.

The Twin Flame's story originates from much further back in history, and the most popular one can be found in the Symposium by the philosopher Plato dated c. 385-370 BC. He states that originally there were 72,000 humans created by the gods, and they each had four arms, four legs, two faces on a single head, and two sets of genitalia.

These original humans were hugely powerful and threatened the gods, who briefly considered eradicating them and consigning humankind to history. They soon realized that if they obliterated humankind, they would also lose their workforce. Humans were the biggest source of energy, and the gods needed to keep them around.

Zeus solved the problem by splitting the humans into two forms. In doing so, he was doubling the workforce and improving the production rate by 100%. The humans lost their power and became mere slaves to the gods. However, they felt the trauma of losing their "other half" deeply and felt they couldn't survive in their current form. They starved themselves and died.

The gods realized that something had to be done, but they didn't want to give the humans their original powers and risk being overpowered. Apollo took charge and devised a way of stitching the two halves together but diminishing their original desires. The result was the human form we know today, with just a belly button remaining from the original physique. Each human had just one set of genitalia but would forever be filled with a desire to reunite with their original other half or their twin flame.

What are Soulmates?

Soulmates are often described as the epitome of love and partnership. As we travel through our different reincarnations, we encounter souls who are part of our soul family. They will appear in your life when you need them, and they will help you make important decisions and become a more enlightened soul in your current life. Some of these souls will become your partner, while some will be friends. Others can be mentors or important people who influence your life. The difference between soulmates and twin flames is the journey you take together.

You have only one twin flame, but you can have multiple soulmates. With twin flames, you will have conflict and go through different stages until you achieve the perfect connection. Soulmates should create less conflict and more love. They can be in your life for decades, or they can stick around for a week or so. Soulmates connect with you instantly. You will feel an instant and overwhelming bond, and your psyche will feel elevated for as long as these people are in your life.

Not everybody gets to meet their twin flame or soulmate. This is because we, as part of society, tend to settle. When we have a good relationship, it's tempting to stay in that relationship because we fear being alone. When we marry or have children or even buy a property together, couples will often stay together even though they know they can do better.

Some of these relationships are necessary to close out a karmic chapter, but most are fueled by the need for companionship. It's difficult to understand what role certain people are supposed to play in your life, and it's crucial to know when to end certain pairings. Uncomfortable questions must be asked. Are the people we are with now our true soulmates, or are they merely filling a gap?

How Do You Recognize a Soulmate?

1) There is inner turmoil: The second you meet a soulmate, your gut will know. It is difficult to explain what happens, but your emotions will be turned on in a way they have never been before.

2) Déjà vu: Soulmates travel with you along your spiritual journey, and you may experience flashbacks that include them. Your meeting may be a mirror image of a previous encounter, and you can feel a shiver of recognition. They will probably feel

the same, and you will use this connection to form your bond in the life you are living.

3) You complete each other: Have you ever met a couple who synch? They finish each other's sentences and work effortlessly as a team. If the experience is with friends or family, it signifies a meeting of soul family members, but if it happens with a partner, then that's your soulmate!

4) You love their flaws: Traditionally, couples recognize that their partner isn't perfect, and they try to "improve them." Maybe they encourage them to diet or change their dress sense. The bottom line is they aren't happy with every aspect of their personality or looks. Soulmates celebrate each other's foibles and quirks. They live with each other no matter what tendencies they have.

5) Intensity: Soulmates know they can overcome any barrier or obstacle that occurs within their relationship. They won't give up and will battle together to get past even the worst moments ever.

6) You act as a team: As a couple, you may be vastly different, but you have that connection, so you compromise. Your soulmate won't necessarily share all your interests, but they will join in to keep you happy. This is a relationship based on unity and balance.

7) You cannot be separated: Circumstances may part you, but mentally you will stay connected. Life may be distancing you from your soulmate, but you will stay connected in your mind. Both of you may pick up the phone to ring each other simultaneously. You could also plan a trip to somewhere that your soulmate is also planning to visit.

8) You feel protected: Despite gender, your soulmate will always be your guardian angel. They have your best interests at heart and will defend you to the death. This is a common way to distinguish if your relationship is based on a soulful connection. If

your current partner has ever made you feel insecure, then they aren't your soulmate.

9) Life without them would be unbearable: Relationships are notoriously difficult to end, and someone will always get hurt. The difference with soulmate relationships is that living apart is inconceivable. The bond you have is worth fighting for, and you will both try everything possible to maintain it.

10) You look each other in the eye: Soulmates have a deep-seated connection and will seal their bond with eye contact. There is a high level of comfort and ease, and when you connect, it can seem like nobody else exists except the two of you.

What are the signs you have a twin flame even though you may not have met yet?

Some people will experience the full cycle of reincarnation with no hint of their twin flame's existence. Others will meet their flame in many different lives and form intense relationships with them. Then there are the souls that know they have a twin flame but aren't destined to meet them physically.

Precursor signs or hints can signal that your true soul half is out there and trying to connect.

These are some common signs that your twin flame is out there somewhere:

• You have never fully committed to a romantic relationship: You may have been part of a couple, but you never really opened your heart to it. Marriage and long-term pairings seem to elude you. This is because you are spiritually involved with your twin flame, and other relationships just don't appeal to you.

• Feeling like a visitor in your environment: If you've ever felt like you don't belong or you feel detached from other people, it could be a sign you need to seek something else. The society you are born into lacks the pull you need to stay, so it may be time to explore other options. Don't worry about where you go because your spiritual twin flame will influence your decisions.

• Feeling different from other people: Do you look at the people you live and work with and feel like they are slightly alien? They don't seem to want the same things you do, or they lack ambition in their life. You could simply yearn for a higher existence that your twin flame offers.

• Spiritual phenomena are strangely appealing: Even if you grew up in a household that focused strictly on corporeal matters and secular beliefs, you feel drawn to spiritual practices. Society often places restrictions on such interests and labels them as dangerous and evil, but you still want to know more. Spirituality is a root of all of us, and if you feel a connection, then explore it and become open to the messages you will receive.

• Places and cultures appeal to you despite no obvious reason: If you experience a need to visit somewhere for no reason, then it could be a sign your flame is connected to that place. It could also mean that in your former life/lives, you and your flame spent time there together. Your twin could be living on a different continent and living in a culture far from your own, so they need you to prepare if you meet.

• You have latent memory of what your ideal partner looks like: Have you ever wondered why some people are drawn to partners with certain hair color or body shape? Why do some women swoon at artistic types while others prefer jocks? This could be because their twin flame had these characteristics in a former life, and your soul remembers them.

• Dreams are vivid and have strangers in them: Do you have a dream participant who strikes a chord when you're asleep, but you have no physical recognition of them? Could this be your twin flame telling you they are around? After all, you need to know what characteristics to look for, so your dreams are the perfect place to connect. These connections can also be intensely spiritual and can feel like your twin has made physical indents into your soul. Some people have described the experience as potent as lovemaking and being held passionately. This is your twin flame connecting on a different plane and signaling how amazing your relationship is even though you're apart.

- The concept of twin flames will repeatedly occur in your consciousness: You may be at a friend's house, and the film "The Notebook" is playing on the TV, or a random article about twin flames suddenly appears in your normal reading matter. The universe is always influencing the path you take, and these subtle signs could mean a meeting is imminent.

- Intense bursts of happiness: Have you ever experienced such elation that your heart feels fit to burst? Deep warm sensations with no apparent reason can mean your twin flame is sending you their loving energy. Accept these feelings and bask in the connection.

- Angel numbers appear in your life: Celestial messages are bound by earthly laws, so some sort of physical sign must replace them. The universe uses Angel numbers to signal their intent and draw our attention toward what they have to say. Most numbers have an angelic meaning, but the more powerful ones are 3, 7, 1, and 2. The master-builder that signals your dreams are about to become real is 22, and if you witness synchronicity including this number, then it could be a message.

Maybe you wake up for no reason at 2.22 am and then fall back to sleep after. If your receipt at the shops contains an unusual sequence like $33.33, this is a message from your twin.

The main difference between soulmate and twin flame relationships is the stages you experience. Soulmates will appear when you need them and disappear when they have accomplished their mission. They can stay around forever, or they will be with you for a relatively short time. Twin flame relationships are different. They have seven distinctive stages that both partners must experience for the process to reach fulfillment.

What are the Seven Stages?

Stage 1: The Search

During this stage of your relationship, you will experience yearning and a feeling of incompleteness. You know that something is missing, and you feel that meeting "the one" is the only relationship you need. Even if the concept of twin flames or soul mates is foreign to you, deep down, you know a spiritual connection is the only way to satisfy your yearning for love.

During this stage, you will open your mind to new ideas. Reading spiritual articles or books will help you discover how to heal and prepare yourself for your twin. Engaging with a therapist or seeking closure from past relationships will help you clear your psyche, ready for the arrival of your flame.

Stage 2: Glimpsing and Meeting

This stage is when you get a physical idea of what your flame looks like. This can be in dreams or real life. The sense of wonder and amazement will be overwhelming as you feel the presence of the Beloved. When you do meet on a physical plane, you will fall hard for them. You are in the best relationship ever, and it is a fairytale coupling that will endure any hardship. Sometimes described by regular couples as the honeymoon period, this goes way beyond that! This is the honeymoon period crossed with a lottery win on steroids. You are in love, and you are bulletproof.

Stage 3: The Testing

At this point, you realize just how alike you both are. Soulmates can differ completely from you with polar opposite personalities, but twin flames are your other half. They will mirror your personality and push you to your limits. As stage 3 progresses, you both contemplate the future and how you can live together in harmony with all the obstacles society throws in your way. Some couples will crumble at this stage and may need to reincarnate together.

Stage 4: The Crisis

This is the stage when your emotions will be put to the ultimate test. Egos will flare, and old wounds will be reopened. Remember, your twin shares all your deepest needs, desires, and dreams, but they also mirror your emotions. For instance, if you are emotionally repressed, they can be explosive with conflict. If they are opinionated, you will probably be shy and quiet, and they can dominate you and push you into uncomfortable situations. This stage is painful and can be devastating for some.

Stage 5: The Runner and Chaser

Following the crisis stage, it is common for a split to happen. One partner will decide that they have had enough, and they will flee their partner. This could be a mutual agreement to spend time apart or a decision by one partner to call time permanently on the relationship. During this game of cat and mouse, the soul's maturity plays a major part in determining the individual's roles.

The partner who chooses to run will often have a less mature soul, while the chaser will be more likely to try and make amends and keep the relationship alive. The runner will sometimes leave for years and cut off all communications before reappearing in their partner's life to try to rekindle the relationship.

Stage 6: Surrender and Dissolution

Now is the time for self-examination and healing. Surrendering is used in this way to describe the process of losing the need to control the relationship. Both parties will work together to understand the issues that led to the crisis and running stage. Both of you will "surrender" your relationship to the universe and realize that destiny will govern how your future maps out.

Stage 7: Oneness

Also called the joining phase, this is when you become a complete unit and begin your mutual journey. At this stage, some partnerships will realize what the world has in store for them. They will see a common goal and work together to achieve it. Empathy and kindness will be the emotions that replace resentment or anger. The couple will become one, and the past will be assigned to the trash.

While these seven stages of twin flame relationships are needed, it can often take several lives and identities to progress through them. Stages can be repeated an infinite number of times until both souls are in the right place and have the required maturity to pass them. The force of awakening is complicated, and not everyone will achieve the process. The key thing to remember is if you do achieve oneness, there is no better experience on Earth or in the spiritual world.

Chapter 8: Rebirth in Astrological Readings

Astrology provides us with one of the most accurate ways of exploring our past lives. Birth charts, also known as natal charts, allow us to see the karmic influences that have traveled with us into our present incarnation. An accurate reading will tell us what form we occupied in former lives and the problems and talents we inherited.

You must believe in astrology as a science and has faith in the importance of reincarnation and past lives to make the process work. Your natal chart will explain different aspects of the life you lead today and why you feel connections to strangers and unknown places. There are several approaches to reading your natal chart, and the first question to ask yourself is, "What is it that excites me about my past lives?"

What is a natal chart, and with what information should you construct it?

At first glance, a natal chart can seem like a complicated graphic image with multiple components that are baffling. Formed in a circle, it is an artistic interpretation of your birth information that is a roadmap to your psyche. When studied correctly, it gives you a wealth of information about every side of your personality. Your good points and weaknesses, whom you love and why you love them, your behavioral traits, and your passions are all mapped in the chart and can expand your vision of your life.

The indispensable data you need are:

- Your forename
- Birthdate
- Gender
- The hour you were born
- Where you were born, geographically, accurately as possible

Some of this information may be unavailable but try and be as accurate as possible. The birth hour can be out by a few minutes, but precision will give you a more accurate reading. Your birth town can also be approximated if the exact location isn't available. If the hour and geographic information aren't provided, you will still get a chart, but it will lack houses.

Depending on the method you choose to use, your chart will now form and create interesting connections. The two most common methods are Koch and Placidus, the latter named after the monk that developed it. Placidus is the default system used for centuries and is considered de rigor by expert astronomers.

The day of the week you were born is a strong indicator of your personality because the planet linked to that day will be amplified in your Natal Chart.

The Days of the Week and Their Correspondences

Monday is the day of the Moon

Tuesday is the day of Mars

Wednesday is the day of Mercury

Thursday is the day of Jupiter

Friday is the day of Venus

Saturday is the day of Saturn

Sunday is the day of the Sun

What this means will be highlighted within your chart.

Within your chart are certain houses that hold the key to details of your past reincarnations. It is essential to understand what disclosures you can expect each house to give.

- The 4th house is the source of ancestral facts. It will reveal details of your roots and the customs and traditions that have followed you into your present incarnation. If you are inclined to favor items or rituals from certain cultural sources, this could be the source of that information and the ties you feel.

- The 8th house is the source of rebirth. It signals the transformation you will have experienced following the events that happened to you during your past lives.

- The 9th house will explain your karmic destiny in the life you are currently living.

- The 12th house is possibly the most important. It tells of the karma from all your former reincarnations and gives a complete picture of your karmic debt and progress.

Planets

The next step is to consider the planets associated with the different houses. You will need to examine both positive and retrograde planets stated in your natal chart as they all have meaning. The positive planetary connections will give you answers to different questions and focus on these areas:

- Mercury: relates to areas of communication and conveying. It indicates you have strong ties with your family and friends and that you have strong sharing skills.

- Venus relates to your relationships, especially marriage and partnership. It highlights your love life and the strength of your ties to material wealth.

- Mars relates to your personal energy and the level of vitality you possess. It also relates to negative energies that have followed you to this plane from former lives.

- Jupiter relates to your level of social development and evolution. Jupiter also indicates the importance you place on your social life and circle of friends.

- Saturn relates to your social maturity and how you handle figures of authority. It signals your preference to spend time with older people and indicates a more mature soul.

Weak planetary connections can be just as informative as strong ones. The positive picture is misleading if it isn't offset by a negative report.

What the weak planet's signal:

- If the Sun is weak in your chart, this means that your former incarnations were likely to have been unfaithful in their relationships and didn't take their duties seriously. Weak sun connections also indicate abuse of power and sinful actions.

- A weak Moon in your horoscope means you didn't respect other people. You played with their emotions and treated them badly. You didn't just take things that weren't yours. You polluted the atmosphere you shared with them.

- Weak Mars connections suggest a permanent rage in your past life. You were selfish and refused to help others. You considered yourself better than others and had no respect for anyone.

- A weak Mercury connection in your horoscope shows emotional immaturity. You considered older people to be past their best and not worthy of your consideration. Environmental issues passed you by, and you probably destroyed a lot of trees and lakes.

- If Jupiter is weak, this signals a huge ego. Your past lives have been spent pursuing your own pleasures and ignoring your spiritual development.

- Weak Venus connections mean you were deceptive and cunning. Theft, fraud, and other underhand methods of behavior will have come easily to you.

- Negative or weak Saturn connections show a tendency to be haughty and aloof. You may have been in positions of power, but you had no empathy with your subordinates and workforce.

The South Node is one of the most important aspects of your natal chart with your past lives. It forms a correlation with your North Node to become your Lunar Nodes. Your North Node tells you who you should be in this life, while your South Node tells you how to move past the mistakes and bad habits you have accumulated. If you don't, you will get nowhere in life and will be stuck in a never-ending cycle of negativity.

What your South Node means to you will become clear once you identify what zodiac sign is your South and North Node.

Aries (March 21 – April 19)

Aries South Nodes means you are self-centered and need to be the center of attention. You are ruthless and will step on others to achieve your needs. To improve, you need to become more sympathetic to other people and help them achieve their dreams. Make friends rather than enemies.

Taurus (April 20 – May 20)

You embrace materialism and have spent your past lives pursuing wealth. Luxury and pleasure were the forces that drove you, and you had no interest in spiritual matters. Now is the time to change your focus and let go of materialistic pleasures and pursuits.

Gemini (May 21 – June 20)

If your South Node is fixed in Gemini, you were dishonest, untrustworthy, and pretty much a constant liar. You were adept at using lies to get yourself out of tricky situations without having to be accountable. You had the gift of the gab but were traitorous. To improve, you must start telling the truth and being more productive and helpful.

Cancer (June 21 – July 22)

If Cancer is your South Node, then you have been a bit of a doormat in the past. Other people have exploited your kind nature and abused your friendship. You take things too personally and fear upsetting others with your opinions.

To improve, you must become more focused on yourself and your life. Give help to others, but only when you have made sure your own needs are met.

Leo (July 23 – August 22)

You allow yourself to take the blame for other people. Other people's problems are like a magnet to you, and you need to stop meddling. Your South Node is telling you to focus more on yourself and sorting out your own problems instead.

Virgo (August 23 – September 22)

The South Node in Virgo means you tend to overanalyze everything. When distracted by small details and irrelevant facts, you fail to see the bigger picture. You need more peace and stability in your life, and you need to heal yourself. Let go of your need to control others and focus on yourself.

Libra (September 23 – October 22)

In past lives, you have been in the limelight and welcomed the attention that others give you. Now is the time to become more rounded and stop seeking gratification from your peers. You need to develop your sense of worth and know your strengths.

Scorpio (October 23 – November 21)

In the past, you have been possessive and manipulative, especially in relationships. You have treated other people badly, and it's time to make amends. Stop relying on other people to make your life better and become more self-sufficient. Only then can you enjoy relationships that are healthy and successful.

Sagittarius (November 22 – December 21)

Your South Node Sagittarius connection tells you that your past lives have been lived unrealistically. You drifted through life without establishing roots and security. Stop living the life of a dreamer and running from life. Adventures are fine, but you need to become more realistic and conform to regular society.

Capricorn (November 22 – January 21)

In past lives, you have been materialistic. You have worked hard to get what you wanted, but you have neglected other people. You have measured happiness by bank statements and personal wealth. Let go of your materialistic tendencies and find happiness in more spiritual ways. Find love and discover your place in society to find true contentment and happiness.

Aquarius (January 22 – February 21)

Your past incarnations have been wary of showing their emotions. You have been bottling things up for too long. Start sharing your feelings no matter how uncomfortable it makes you feel. Let your emotions out, and you will make different choices in life and become part of a social group free to speak and loves to share.

Pisces (February 22 – March 21)

South node in Pisces indicates that you lack the strength to stand up for yourself. You have been guilty of lacking self-worth, so it's time to change. Stop letting people take advantage of you and learn the word no. Put yourself first and only help others when they are genuinely in need.

How can I get an astral chart?

You can consult a professional astrologer by visiting Kasamba.com, an online site that currently lists 93 online astrology reading advisors who will give you a detailed natal chart for varying prices. The site also tells you what to expect and offers a less detailed free version of the chart.

Other online resources include astrology.com and astrolibrary.org.

Here is a sample of the results of a free chart created for a male named John, born Jan 14th in New York at 6.14 am.

The planets and points in the signs include Sun in Capricorn, which indicates that John is conservative, honest, and efficient. Yet, he can be worried and pessimistic. He is best suited to careers that require integrity and organization.

The ascendant in Capricorn indicates he may have had trouble communicating in his early life, and he suffers from the fear of inadequacy. Because John is reserved, he can come across as cold and unfeeling, which can manifest in physical pain, especially in the knee area. The spiritual lesson to learn is to lighten up and become more sociable.

Johns North Node is in Cancer, which indicates that he will become more assured and comfortable in his own skin as he ages. He will gravitate to positions of authority and seek to contribute to society. In the first house, the sun and moon back up the tendency for John to be prone to mood swings, and he can lack confidence.

Mercury in the first and twelfth house suggests John suffers from nerves and anxiety when faced with social situations, resulting in his slim stature. His nerves don't hold him back, but they do speed up his metabolism.

Mars in the first house means he has an energy that can lead to recklessness. Sometimes his sensible persona will be cast aside, and he will throw caution to the wind and do something reckless. Uranus in the eighth house suggests psychic abilities and keen intuition.

John has strong ideas about sex and death, and he believes in reincarnation and sustaining relationships in successive lives. The afterlife is a great mystery to him, and he will explore occult ideas and more conventional ones. Uranus in the eighth house is also a sign of spiritual healing powers, and John may be blessed with the power of laying on hands.

Saturn in the second house means John is careful with his money. He understands the importance of having savings, but he can sometimes forget to enjoy the fruits of his labor. There has been too much focus on materialism in former lives, and this can cause depression and fear of poverty in this life. He must learn to achieve a healthy balance and share his possessions and wealth with others.

Neptune in the eleventh house is elusive and means John is prone to indecision. He attracts bohemian types with weird and wacky ideas and tends to work in the creative sector. They may try and introduce him to hallucinogens or alcohol to "expand his mind," but he will have the strength to resist.

Johns North Node is in the seventh house, which tells him he must stop looking at the world with a blinkered view. He needs to develop a wider scope and discover what he's capable of. His past lives have had slight progress, but now is the time to gain confidence and enthusiasm. He should stop seeking gratification from others and trust his own opinion instead.

The extracts from the natal chart of John are just part of the information contained in the free reading from astrolibrary.com. There is a detailed chart with detailed components and links to other sources of information that help explain what it all means. You need not be an expert to read the chart. You just need the patience to study it.

The site also offers daily transit reports, which are like a horoscope but more detailed, and a couple's compatibility report. This is a synastry report that gives astrological indications of compatibility for couples. This report is based on how the sun and the planets align but not the moon, so it doesn't require a birth time. It is incredibly detailed and describes how couples need to adapt and what areas of their lives will be subject to both conflict and love.

Don't be put off by the terms used within these types of charts. They are detailed and contain information about past lives and the present. They offer an insightful view into an individual or couples' relationship with other people. There are health and career suggestions in the charts that may surprise you and cause you to rethink your current situation.

The bottom line is if you are invested in the spiritual side of your life or lives, then you will understand how the astral plane influences everything and everybody. If you believe, then why wouldn't you look at natal charts to discover what they can tell you? Modern online resources mean that the results are just a few clicks away. Even if you are skeptical, what harm can it do to check out what the stars have in store for you?

Chapter 9: See Your Past Lives

Reincarnation has now been identified as part of your soul's history, so the next step is to examine what happened in your former lives. Seeking help from a professional is the obvious choice for some, and regression therapy is widely available from qualified therapists. If the thought of therapy is alien to you, it can help to know how the therapy works.

Regression Therapy Explained

Most patients seek this form of therapy to treat phobias, depression, or other debilitating concerns. Therapists work with them to uncover past experiences that have influenced their current lives and relive them to come to terms with the effects they had. Experts have used hypnotherapy and psychoanalysis for decades to delve into the past and solve current issues and conflicts.

Freud was a major influencer in this field of therapy and believed that his patients' childhood traumas were the key to treating adult disorders. Modern regression therapy treatments still refer to his ideas as they take the therapy one step further and delve into past lives and incarnations. In the 1980s, leading psychiatrist Brian Weiss developed further techniques that catapulted regression therapy into becoming a credited form of treatment.

The therapy works on three levels of consciousness. The central components focus on these areas of thought:

- The conscious mind. This focuses on thoughts that the patient clearly remembers or has memories about.

- The subconscious mind. Focusing on emotions that the patient has no memory of. These emotions and instincts are buried in the mind, and the therapist will use different techniques to release them.

- The superconscious mind. Spiritually this part of the human psyche is known as the soul. This higher level of consciousness is the place intentions and dreams lie. It is a platform for how the patient wants to develop.

Past life regression helps us heal in our current life and works in the following way.

Preparation

This is the first stage of therapy and involves a mild hypnotic state being invoked. The patient will be asked to lie down on a couch and close their eyes. They will be asked to imagine a set of stairs to go down slowly while counting to ten. Verbal cues will help them relax as they descend, and when they reach the bottom, they will be hypnotized.

Regression Techniques

Different therapists use varying ways to take their patients to an astral plane. Most will place thoughts in a familiar environment by creating a familiar starting point. They will identify what all the senses are feeling and ask the patient to drink in their surroundings.

Now they will ask for help from a spiritual guide that the patient believes in. This could be an angel, spirit guide, or any other ethereal being. Now the journey back in time begins.

Expressing Emotions and Exploring the Life Lived

As the patient reaches their past incarnation, the therapist will ask pertinent questions. What does the client see when they look at their feet and hands? What age are they? What is their occupation? The therapist will gently probe the sensations, intensity, and emotions the client is feeling and their story.

This process can access different lives within one session or deal with one life per session. Therapists' methods are based on their clients' ability to cope with the intense emotions that can be released, and they will always be aware of the patient's safety.

Reprogramming the Subconscious Mind

Now the therapy will focus on changing the core emotions affecting the patient today. They will use positive self-imagery and talk to dispel negative influences brought forward from the past. These emotions and memories can act as roadblocks to success, and it is the therapist's job to remove them. Fear can often play a part in the lack of confidence as the human body is hardwired to face fear and survive at all costs.

If former lives have included traumas and experiences that heighten fear levels, therapy can be used to move past these fears and put them in perspective. It is difficult to create change in current life if the mental lesions from past lives aren't healed.

Ending the Session

The client needs to return to the "real world" comfortably. Therapists will bring the patient back to reality with gentle counting back with reassuring words.

Some therapists will dispute that using hypnosis is the best way to regress subjects. They are concerned that the technique can be subject to "false memories." They prefer to use a method called the Quantum Healing Technique, where the subject is placed in a semi somnambulistic state that allows them to forget about their physical body and explore their mind.

The subject is encouraged to hold real conversations with their former incarnations and ask questions about their lives. Practitioners believe this form of therapy is more exploratory than hypnosis and encourage their subjects to ask practical questions and spiritual ones. They believe the wisdom of their former selves will give them a greater insight into the workings of the universe and reincarnation. Some people describe the process as being able to check out the documentation of their soul's journey.

What if the thought of seeing a therapist leaves you cold? Someone poking about in your personal thoughts and memories and having free reign over your memories is not for everybody, so it may be better for you to explore your past lives alone. You are better placed to deal with the facts and details you will uncover and call a halt to proceedings when you feel the need.

Being in control of your expanded consciousness means you are in control at all times. The potential for exploration is immense, and the process is relatively simple. You can personalize the experience to ensure you have the greatest chance of success.

How to Regress Yourself and Reconnect with Your Past Lives

Before you begin the physical process takes some time to gather things that will help you regress. If you feel a sense of déjà vu whenever you smell certain aromas, then make sure you can smell them when you regress. If you feel a pull whenever France is mentioned, make sure you have visual representations of Gallic life.

Pictures of the Eiffel tower or a bottle of red wine will help trigger memories from the region.

Step 1 Prepare the Room

Choose the room you will use to perform the process and place the triggers in the line of sight. Now make sure the temperature is correct, cool but not cold. Clear the room of distractions and close the curtains to block out light. The room should be lit with ambient lights and soothing colors. Use noise to guide yourself to former lives, like the sound of the beach or other sounds that appeal to your psyche.

Crystals and spiritual symbols can enhance the process, so make sure they are within your reach or sight if you need reassurance. Images of spiritual symbols will help you feel safe as you begin your journey to the past. Whatever makes you feel protected works and makes sure you encounter only good energy.

Step 2: Prepare Yourself

Sometimes we can forget to do obvious tasks when focusing on something potentially life-changing, but our body should be in optimum shape. Have eaten a light meal and hydrated yourself before you start the process, or you could be distracted by your hunger and thirst.

Your clothing should be comfortable and loose. Cool cotton shifts and loose-fitting yoga pants are ideal. You may feel a pull from a former life to dress a certain way, and that's great; any form of influence will only make the journey smoother. Whatever clothing appeals to you should be used. You may have a pair of ballet shoes you loved despite never learning how to dance or a Stetson you think is great; just go with it; nobody is judging you.

Step 3: Meditate and Become More Mindful

You need to improve your focus and become more receptive to the path you are about to take. While you may know how you lived in your former incarnations, there will probably be some surprises ahead. Preparing yourself is a key part of this process, and meditation will clear your mind of unwanted clutter, so it is ready for your new information.

Doing self-regression is not something you do lightly. The process might lead to disturbing or upsetting revelations about your former incarnations. We know there are bad people in the world, and you probably may have been a deeply unpleasant character in a past life. You need to be prepared for this eventuality and begin the process with a healthy mindset and attitude.

Meditation isn't a cure-all, but it can give you incredible benefits both physically and spiritually when combined with the extra steps listed here. All you need are patience, kindness, and self-compassion – oh, and a comfortable place to sit!

- Take a seat in a place that is calm, peaceful, and free from distractions.

- Set your time limit.

- Become aware of your body, feel your toes and feet on the floor, and allow your thoughts to travel up until they reach the top of your head.

- Breathe deeply and visualize what happens as your breath fills your lungs and then escapes through your mouth.

- Has your mind wandered? While you were contemplating your body and breath, what happened to your thoughts? Take a moment to discover what your mind is doing, and then return to your breathing exercise.

- Embrace the path your mind has taken. Don't judge or obsess about the thoughts your mind has conjured up. Just let it be.

- Now close with kindness. Grant yourself a period to come back to reality. Gently open your eyes and notice the physical environment you are in. As you return, note your emotions and feelings post-meditation.

Step 4: Protect Yourself with Light

Your physical-spiritual symbols and items will provide you with a level of protection, but you can always benefit from extra levels of safety. You need to guard against negative energy and cleanse the obstructive forces that may lie in your path.

Lie on the floor in the room you have chosen to perform the process and close your eyes. Place your arms by your side and breathe deeply until you feel fully relaxed. Imagine an enveloping white light closing around your feet and traveling up your body. Feel the warmth and security it brings and surrender yourself to it.

Remember, this light is your cloak of protection against negative forces and energies. It will cocoon you with its love, and you will feel elevated and fulfilled. Chanting powerful mantras will make the light stronger and brighter. Phrases like "I am filled with love, and I feel the protective aura wash over me" or "This light is the ultimate protection, and it will travel with me on my journey of enlightenment" will help you feel secure and part of the spiritual energy your words represent.

Experiment with different colors to energize the light and customize it to your needs. Return to white, repeat, and return. There is no time limit to this stage. You may get it the first time, or you may need to practice. Once you feel 100% protected, you will know it's time for the next step.

Step 5: Begin Your Journey

Now you will need to visualize your path. Imagine a long hallway with a door at the end. This can be a familiar hallway from your physical reality, or it can be one your mind has conjured. Take a long hard look at it and commit every detail to memory. You need to remember it in detail because this is the portal to your past lives. The door at the end is a direct link to your former personas, and use it every time you need to visit a past life.

Step 6: Take the First Step

Once you have committed the hallway to memory, it's time to walk down toward your door. Make every step count. This is a momentous undertaking you are embarking on, so treat the process with the respect it deserves. What does the hallway smell of? How does it feel underfoot? Is it carpeted, or does it have floorboards? Are there any sounds, or can you just hear your own footsteps? Give the process your full attention and drink in the sensations you are feeling.

When you do reach the door, take a deep breath and take hold of the doorknob. Don't rush to open the door; prepare yourself mentally and physically. Once the bolt is disengaged, breathe deeply and give it a gentle push.

Step 7: Enter the Past

Nothing can prepare you for what lies beyond the door. It can be a wall of color, a pastoral scene, a portrayal of an historical event, or just a field. It doesn't matter; what you see before you are merely a foundation for your mind from which to launch itself. Embrace the experience and become enveloped in the vision. Your mind will now take charge and direct you to the place you need to be. It can feel like a dream for some people, while it can seem like the most vivid reality they have encountered for others.

Step 8: Be Patient

The process is different for everyone, and you may feel disappointed after your first attempt. The door could have opened to reveal absolutely nothing and see this as a failure. No journey down the hallway is a complete failure. You may have been underprepared, so return to reality and think about how you could enhance the process. Are there any key triggers you overlooked?

Maybe you see just mist as the door opens. Try the shoe method to clarify what you see. As you stand at the entrance, take a glimpse toward your feet and note your footwear. Are they your regular shoes, or do you see something new? Sandals could indicate Roman times, and shiny boots could mean a military background. Once you identify the footwear, let your gaze rise and notice the rest of your outfit.

Always begin your next session with the images you have seen already. Elevate your thoughts from a known source and increase the chance of success at discovering an unknown source.

Step 9: Acknowledge What You See

We all have analytical thoughts, and the process you are experiencing goes against everything you believed formerly. That you are interested in connecting with former incarnations means that some barriers have been lowered. Now it's time to believe in the unbelievable. What you experience is all in the past and is unchangeable, so it's time to accept what you see.

Ask yourself how you feel about what you are undergoing. Is it real for you, or are you convinced it's all a dream or the product of an overactive imagination? Only you can decide and what to do next. You need to believe that what you see is a genuine representation of your former lives, or you will never progress.

Step 10: Return to the Present

This step will normally happen with no effort. Your mind will decide when you have experienced enough, and it's time to go. The vision will fade, and the images will disappear as your analytical mind regains control.

You can engineer your departure by retracing your steps in the hallway. Close the door, turn around and return to the starting point you recognize.

Freewriting

Another tool to use for exploring your former lives is freewriting. Professional writers use it to generate thoughts and ideas when suffering from writer's block, but the habit can help you create text about your experiences with reincarnation.

Think of a prompt that resonates with your idea of how you lived in the past. This can be a person who appears in your dreams or a prominent place in your recollections. Now write about them. Focus your mind and use pen and paper or a computer to record your freewriting. Change how you write about the subject you have chosen, talk about them as a secondary character or write as if they are the subject of a first-person narrative.

Prompts aren't limited to physical levels. Emotions can trigger some incredible text and experiences, so focus on what type of emotion you feel when you consider your former lives. Do you feel sad, elated, or simply curious? Write about what those emotions mean to you and how they manifest.

If you need some inspiration or help to aid your freewriting technology can come to your aid. There are many writing prompts online to help, and they will give you immediate inspiration whenever you need it. Try the <u>Writer's Digest</u> or download an app like <u>Write About</u> to get the process started.

Chapter 10: Shamanic Reincarnations

Shamanism has been a part of society since man first inhabited the Earth. It is sometimes called the first religion, but as a modern concept, shamanism has become a more flexible term that describes a belief system with the shaman as the central figure. Shamans were an important part of society when medicines and traditional healing methods weren't widely available. They used their powers to heal people and provide them with a way to communicate with the spiritual world.

Modern shamanism has adapted and changed to suit the societies that still believe in the shaman's power. Contacting spirits is still a central concept in shamanic practices, but different rites are used by cultures depending on their contact and influences from modern sciences.

Today, modern society has seen an increase in the interest in shamanism, and the term neo-shamanism has become a common way to describe the notions contained in practice. As alternative healing and therapy are experiencing a surge in popularity, practitioners are incorporating the doctrines and magical teachings of shamanism and adjusting them to suit their needs.

Millions of people worldwide have turned to shamanism to seek comfort and wisdom, and all shamans are governed by a set of core beliefs that align them with the principles of the practice.

The Seven Core Beliefs of Shamanism

1) Everyone and everything is connected. The physical and spiritual worlds are all connected and follow a pattern designed by the powers that govern us all.

2) There is an alternate reality known by different terms depending on the cultural influences. This world is sometimes called a dream world by modern shamans.

3) Not everybody will have the belief or power to access this alternate reality, and therefore they need shamans. Only those with an overwhelming desire to travel to the spiritual world will do so. When they do, they will be gifted with healing powers and the wisdom to solve others' problems.

4) There is a hierarchy of healers and teachers who reside in an alternate reality. The spirits and godlike residents represent a range of religions and beliefs. The Siberian form of shamanism tells of 4 main deities named Tengri, Ulgen, Umai, and Erlik, who rule the four corners of the universe, while other versions of shamanism show Jesus as one of the main teachers and spiritual leaders.

5) The belief that everything has a soul. Animate or inanimate beings are all blessed with a spiritual soul and have a mindful existence.

6) There is a life force that drives all animate beings. This is described as the chi in Chinese culture and the baraka in Muslim teachings.

7) The life force comes with a personal force that emanates around the body. In Eastern teachings, this is classed as a person's aura and is directly connected to the energy centers within the body known as chakras or meridians.

Shamanic Journeys

Some practices focus on the shaman's ability to take soul journeys of exploration for the people who sought their help. Shamans were often initiated because they had experienced some form of trauma that led to them experiencing a soul journey like a near-death experience. It was common for shamans to have experienced the soul leaving their body, which led to the power to duplicate the experience and direct their soul to take the journey required.

The destination of these journeys differs depending on the cultural influences. There is a map to the shamanic universe containing three levels interjoined by a central axis called the World Tree.

This belief system is called shamanic cosmology, and the archetypal worlds within are regarded as the common psychological inheritance of humanity. Mankind didn't invent this cosmology. It is a part of the human psyche woven into the matrix. This is true, whatever we believe or acknowledge. It simply is.

The Shamans Universe

The three planes of consciousness are the Upper World, the Middle World, and the Lower World.

The Upper World is also called the Celestial realm, and this is where the spiritual echelon resides. Many outcomes to situations and experiences exist here, and the shaman travels to this world to find quintessential knowledge they can bring back to reality to influence the natural world.

This reality contains a blueprint for humanity and has infinite possibilities for healing the world. The shaman will journey to this realm when they feel there is an imbalance on Earth that can only be solved by interaction with the revered beings who reside in the Upper Realm. Humans are notorious for creating disharmony and straying from the ordained pattern of the universe.

The Middle world is a parallel universe that mirrors our reality. There are no physical beings on this level, simply the spirits that represent them. Imagine a world that appears to be a duplicate of the physical world inhabited by the trues forms of people and things we know on Earth. Travel in this world is effortless and involves belief and love. The shaman can cover great distances with just a single thought, and their journeys will be fueled by the desire to seek knowledge.

Spirit journeys in this realm are filled with communication between souls and spirits. Deep and meaningful information and philosophies are shared with visitors, and the links formed there can travel back to the physical world and provide the shaman with a network of people to work with.

The Lower world is the realm the human soul travels to following physical death. It holds the spirits of animals, humans, and designated spirit guides and is regarded as the powerful source of power for ailing souls. This journey is called soul retrieval and is part of the healing process a soul can undergo when it retreats from the physical world.

More conventional reincarnation beliefs involve the growth and healing of the soul while residing in earthly form. Shamanic teachings believe that parts of the soul become wounded on Earth and need a place to retreat and recover. This is the place they retreat to, and shamans will often journey to the Lower world to guide them back to the remnants they left on Earth.

The World Tree is the axis that connects the three realms, and shamans have the power to traverse these realms using the power of drumming. The World Tree responds to rhythmic drumming that originates from drums made of the original material wood. There is a bridge formed by the soundwaves that form a tunnel. This leads directly to the World Tree and forms a tunnel through which they can pass freely. Passage through the tunnel can be multi-directional. As shamans pass, so do spirits, and if the drumbeats, the entrance remains open.

Shamanic Journeys to Discovery

While the concept of journeying between the three worlds in shamanic cosmology may seem far removed, most people possess the innate skills needed to travel with their souls. It is a deep-seated knowledge that just needs reawakening. You need not be a shaman or have experienced near-death experiences to journey. Modern practitioners recognize the skill as a spiritual tool to explore other realms. They understand that this type of discovery is a powerful way to explore the realms that define the universe without gaining healing powers or other shamanic strengths.

Before you consider if journeying is for you, it is important to understand what happens. Spiritual rites and powers can be daunting and need to be treated with respect. Some numerous modern sources and workshops reputably teach people how to journey through the Worlds and keep you safe.

What Happens When You Journey?

Shamanic-style journeys are generally used to discover the secrets of the physical world and what their bodies are made of. Journeyers can visit guardian spirits who watch over them, or they can explore the health of themselves or others. They can visit the archetypal spirits of the land or the seas and join them as they oversee the natural world.

Some people find the journey is a perfect way to address issues that occurred in the physical world but can't be resolved there. They can confront the souls of the deceased and challenge them about abuse or emotional conflicts in the Lower world where they will feel safe to do so. The journey provides them with a safe platform to work through their anger without causing damage to themselves. Grief is often the emotion that fuels a journey as most living souls regret not saying something to their loved ones who have passed away.

Some journeyers will experience nature in a way that surpasses the physical world. They may travel through the seas in the soul of a dolphin or experience the joy of swimming through the mighty oceans with their companions. They could be running with a herd of gazelles and physically feel the hind legs' force that power the animal's speed. In dreams, we imagine what it's like to run with wild animals or swim with fish. In journeying, we experience it, and it's joyful to discover the mysteries of their anatomy and thought processes.

The places you journey to will differ every time you undertake to travel. They will include diverse options that can appear to look like a magical version of Earth or the Middle world, or they can be as spiritual as a place filled with light and energy. Gravity and other physical conventions don't apply when you journey. The rules of energy and your desires will decide where you visit and give yourself fully to the experience.

Some shamanic journeys take a different path and are rooted in smaller dimensions. They may find themselves enveloped by a grain of sand or a drop of water traveling from the sky to the Earth. Every journey is relevant and has a purpose. Some journeyers will travel extensively and cross swathes of land and air in one session, while others will visit just one or two destinations. As a journeyer becomes more skilled and practiced in the art of traveling, they risk becoming so immersed in their journey they fail to return. This risk can be mitigated by having a person in the physical world who has a "safe word," which will call the traveler back to reality.

How Do You Feel, Physically, When Journeying?

Every experience is different, but they do follow a familiar pattern on Earth. Some people prefer to distance themselves from the room they are in by covering their eyes, while some will have no problem distancing themselves from reality without physical aids.

The impact on the senses of the journeyer will vary immensely. Some experience a vivid connection with the places they visit and describe a multi-color cinematic experience with all-around sounds, smells, and vision crowding their minds, while others will fail to experience some of their senses on their journey. Some travelers describe a sense of leaving their body and seeing the shell of themselves below as they leave the room. Others will feel like their trip took place within their soul, and they didn't need to leave the body.

The sensory way we experience our normal lives is not always the same when journeying. Some people report an experience that wasn't as clear as the others, as if their contact with the spirits was more than ethereal. It can be explained as the sense of knowing someone has entered a room without having the physical or visual evidence to confirm their presence. You just know they are there.

Why Can Some People Journey and Others Cannot?

Shamanic journeying may be an innate part of our psyche, but not everyone can do it. These are some reasons they have trouble journeying:

Reason 1: Mental Detritus

You need to focus on travel a spiritual path. If your mind is filled with chatter and mindless conversations, it's difficult to focus on the experience. When you journey, your soul leaves the room, so it will fail to gather momentum and leave if it is distracted by mental ties. You need to silence or tune out the detritus in your head and form a clear path to success.

Reason 2: The Inability to Let Go of Conventional Thoughts

When you enter the spiritual realm, some strange stuff can happen. No matter how much instruction or how many workshops you attend, you will never be prepared for what happens on your journey. As a functioning human, we need to analyze data and understand what it means, but as a journeyer, we need to leave that analytical process behind. The journey needs to flow, and you need to surrender to the force.

If you get off the track to evaluate elements of your trip, then you interrupt the flow. So, what if a random table appears in the forest you are visiting? Should you know why the eagle you are traveling with is bright purple? Expect the unexpected and embrace the absurdity along with the magical.

Reason 3: High Expectations

We live in a highly visual society, and journeys can often affect other senses without seeing anything. Some people find this disappointing, and they expect an all singing all dancing visual display. Journeys will often happen in a non-visual way, and you need to appreciate the opportunity to use your other senses and experience fewer familiar feelings.

Reason 4: I Just Imagined it All

This is one of the most common obstacles shamanic journeyers stumble on. Their analytic brain dismisses the experiences as just a product of their overactive imagination. Your imagination is constantly analyzing your daily life and interpreting your experiences, so it is normal to think your journey has elements of imagination attached to it. The difference between your imagination and your journey is you will genuinely discover things unknown to you on your trip.

The information you gain on your journey is real. It is given to you, so you can make an impact in your life and on the people that surround you. Your imagination can only work with facts and know elements.

Reason 5: You're Intentions Lack Focus

You need to know why you are embarking on a soul trip, and you need to focus on what your intentions are. Even though we aren't always aware of intentions dictating our actions, they happen every minute. When you make a cup of coffee, your actions are based on an intention. You intend to open a door, and then you do it. If your intentions are unclear, then your journey will be haphazard and unsuccessful.

Advanced journeyers can travel without a clear intention, but early trips need to be fueled by a clear intent. Curiosity about the process is not enough to make your journey successful.

Reason 6: Depleted Battery

When you plan to travel somewhere in your car, you need to know certain parts of your vehicle are working. You check your brakes, oil and water levels, and the amount of fuel in your tank. Most people also check their battery is fully charged.

This journey should be no different. Be hydrated and fed. Your energy levels should be high, and your internal battery should be fully charged and ready to go. Some groups of shamanic societies perform uplifting rituals to raise their energy levels before traveling. They sing and dance with gusto and boost their energy with the physical and spiritual joy of music.

If you are experiencing low energy levels due to ill health or physical reasons, you shouldn't attempt to journey. If your energy is low because of psychological factors, try singing or taking a walk before you start. Some people find it easier to travel in groups, so you may benefit from organized classes or workshops.

Reason 7: Inability to Tune Out

As with mental chatter, extraneous noise can be hard to block out. When you journey, your soul splits, and part of it remains in the physical world. If it is distracted by external sources, it can force the traveling part of the soul to return. Focusing on your soulful journey is like listening to a fascinating radio program. You become engrossed in the broadcast and b lockout other distractions.

Shamanic practices can involve the use of hallucinogens and other mind-altering substances. These are not recommended for beginners and should never be used without expert supervision. If you are looking for a more traditional way to explore your past lives, you can try astral projection. This is a simpler way for the soul to leave the body and explore the astral planes.

How to Astral Project

Stage 1: Enter a State of Deep Relaxation

Meditation or music helps you reach this stage. Close your eyes and relax in a dark atmosphere. Clear your mind and body of all thought and movement, then focus on your breathing. Holding a quartz crystal will help you focus your mind and attract spiritual vibrations.

Stage 2: Become Hypnagogic

You should now be on the edge of sleep. This is the hypnagogic stasis, and it allows the brain to wander. Visualize your hand until it is clear, and your mind is filled with the image. Now move around the body until all mental chatter has left your mind.

Stage 3: Experience the Vibes

At this stage, some people report feeling disturbing vibrations. Strong waves of energy cause vibrations to free the soul from the meditative state. This happens directly before the astral projection is about to happen.

Stage 4: See the Rope

Now it's time to leave your body and explore the room. Use your mind to disconnect your soul and walk to the other side of the room. See your body and acknowledge it is you. Between your soul and the body, there should be a connection. This is sometimes a rope or a silver cord and is used to guide the soul back to the physical body it is currently projecting from.

Stage 5: Explore the Plane

In early sessions, train your mind to return when you need it to. Practice exploring the physical plane by leaving the room and observing objects outside your physical sight. When the soul returns to your body, check that what your projected soul saw is correct.

This stage should be repeated until the process of recall is totally natural and unforced. Remaining on the physical plane may be frustrating, but it is necessary to become comfortable with the process before exploring other spiritual planes. Think of it as learning to walk before you can fly!

Conclusion

Now you know what other people in different cultures believe, you are better placed to form your own opinions. You have the methods and exercises to investigate your past lives and learn what went on before this life. If you always felt a strong pull to all things European, or maybe you rise to your feet when the French national anthem plays, maybe you lived in Europe in a former life. Knowledge is power, and you now have plenty of that and a handy guide to navigate your way through all things related to reincarnation.

Good luck, and remember to stay safe and enjoy the journey!

Here's another book by Mari Silva that you might like

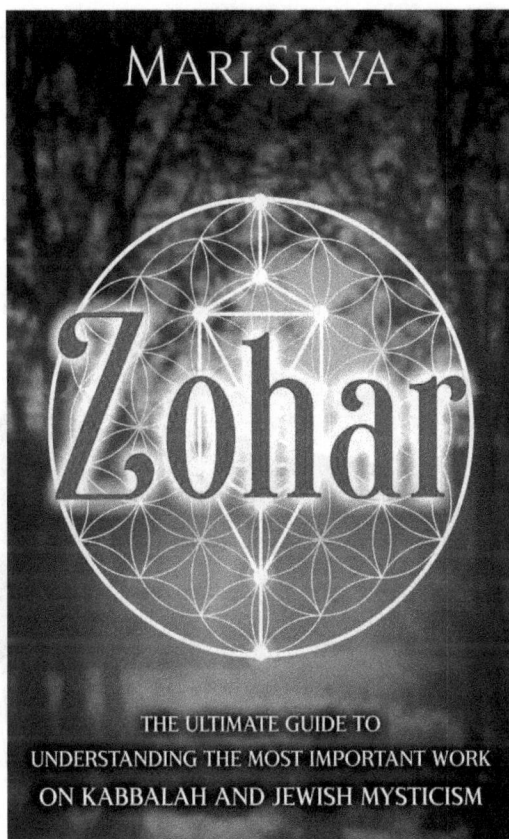

MARI SILVA

Zohar

THE ULTIMATE GUIDE TO
UNDERSTANDING THE MOST IMPORTANT WORK
ON KABBALAH AND JEWISH MYSTICISM

Your Free Gift (only available for a limited time)

Thanks for getting this book! If you want to learn more about various spirituality topics, then join Mari Silva's community and get a free guided meditation MP3 for awakening your third eye. This guided meditation mp3 is designed to open and strengthen ones third eye so you can experience a higher state of consciousness. Simply visit the link below the image to get started.

https://spiritualityspot.com/meditation

References

"6 Things Jews Believe about Reincarnation." Www.beliefnet.com, https://www.beliefnet.com/faiths/judaism/galleries/6-things-jews-believe-about-reincarnation.aspx

"7 Core Beliefs of Shamanism." SHAMAN'S VOICE, 31 Oct. 2017, www.shamansvoice.co.uk/7-core-beliefs-of-shamanism/

"8 Signs You Are an Old Soul Who Has Reincarnated Many Times." Her.womenworking.com, her.womenworking.com/signs-you-are-an-old-soul-reincarnated-many-times-before-rebirth

"8 Twin Flame Stages – Are You Experiencing This?" Mind Journal, 3 July 2020, themindsjournal.com/8-major-twin-flame-stages/2/

"10 Interesting Cases of Supposed Reincarnation." List verse, 21 Oct. 2013, listverse.com/2013/10/21/10-interesting-cases-of-supposed-reincarnation/

"Are You an Old Soul? – 40 Telltale Signs You've Been around Awhile." Spirit Earth Awakening, 17 Nov. 2016, www.spiritearthawakening.com/spirituality/reincarnation/soul-ages/old-soul-40-telltale-signs-youve-around-awhile

"Awakened Soul: The Last Reincarnation ★ LonerWolf." LonerWolf, 16 Jan. 2015, lonerwolf.com/awakened-soul-reincarnation/

barry. "The Seven Soul Types: What Do They Look Like?" Personality & Spirituality, 23 June 2010, personalityspirituality.net/2010/06/23/the-seven-soul-types-what-do-they-look-like/

"BBC - Religions - Paganism: Wicca." Bbc.co.uk, 2014, http://www.bbc.co.uk/religion/religions/paganism/subdivisions/wicca.shtml

Cassady. "20 Signs That You Have a Twin Flame (Even If You've Never Met)." Twin Flames 11:11, 20 Sept. 2019, www.twinflames1111.com/blog/recognition/20-signs-you-have-a-twin/

Crawford, Hayden. "11 Steps to Uncover the Secrets of Your Past Life: Reincarnation." Numerologist.com, 22 Sept. 2018, numerologist.com/spiritual-growth/past-life-reincarnation/

Edwards-Fowle, Lauren, et al. "What Is a Karmic Relationship and 7 Signs You Are in One." Life Advancer, 23 July 2017, www.lifeadvancer.com/karmic-relationship/

"How Does Karma Affect Your Life?" The Chopra Center, 8 Jan. 2016, chopra.com/articles/how-does-karma-affect-your-life

How to Astral Project (Beginner's Guide to Astral Travel). www.psychicgurus.org/how-to-astral-project-safely/

"How to Remember Past Life Memories in 10 Easy Steps." Gaia, www.gaia.com/article/how-access-memories-your-past-lives

https://www.howstuffworks.com/about-author.htm. "How Reincarnation Works." HowStuffWorks, 5 Dec. 2007, people.howstuffworks.com/reincarnation.htm

Jain, Ashutosh. "The Legend of Maitreya &Karma -Yoga." Medium, 17 June 2020, medium.com/indian-thoughts/the-legend-of-maitreya-karma-yoga-a914964bd5a5

Jr, Bill Murphy. "10 Selfless Ways to Build Good Karma and Generate Happiness." Inc.com, 11 Mar. 2015, https://www.inc.com/bill-murphy-jr/10-selfless-ways-to-build-good-karma-and-generate-happiness.html.

Lapik, Elena. "How to Know about Past Life through Astrology by Date of Birth | Astromix.net." Astromix.net / Blog, 7 Apr. 2020, astromix.net/blog/know-past-life/

"Mirror Soul Meaning: Twin Flames Stages and Signs." The Law of Attraction, 15 Oct. 2018, www.thelawofattraction.com/twin-flames/

myspiritualshenanigans, Author. "Karma : 7 Spiritual Facts about the Divine Law of Cause and Effect." My Spiritual Shenanigans, 20 July 2019, myspiritualshenanigans.blog/karma/

"Past Lives - How to Reconnect with Our Past Lives." Goop, 3 Oct. 2019, goop.com/wellness/spirituality/uncovering-past-lives/

PowerofPositivity. "6 Ways to Create Good Karma | Power of Positivity." Power of Positivity: Positive Thinking & Attitude, 3 Feb. 2015, www.powerofpositivity.com/6-ways-to-create-good-karma/

Rae, Dunnea. "9 Ways to Find Past Life Connections through Astrology." Medium, 17 June 2018, alohaastro.medium.com/9-ways-to-find-past-life-connections-through-astrology-bd4e01118e6e

Reincarnation – Learn Kabbalah. learnkabbalah.com/reincarnation/

Reincarnation and Past Lives: The 7 Stages of Death and Birth -. 10 Jan. 2020, newagespirituality.com/reincarnation/

"Reincarnation: The 35 Steps of Soul Evolution." Personality & Spirituality, personalityspirituality.net/articles/the-michael-teachings/reincarnation-the-35-steps/

Sage, Mackenzie. "Wiccan Views on Life after Death." Exemplore, Exemplore, 12 Dec. 2013, exemplore.com/wicca-witchcraft/Wiccan-Views-on-Life-After-Death

"Shamanic Paradigm." Shamanicdrumming.com, shamanicdrumming.com/shamanic_paradigm.html

"Soul Types: The Seven Roles in Essence." Personality & Spirituality, personalityspirituality.net/articles/the-michael-teachings/the-seven-roles-in-essence/

The. "The Origins of Shamanism: Shamanism Beliefs & History." Gaia, 2017, www.gaia.com/article/how-much-do-you-know-about-shamanism

"What Is a South Node in an Astrology Chart, and What Each Zodiac Sign Placement Means • GOSTICA." GOSTICA, 24 June 2019, gostica.com/astrology/south-node-in-an-astrology-chart/

"What Type of Soul Do You Have? Find out with This Personality Quiz." Mind Journal, 23 Aug. 2016, themindsjournal.com/what-type-of-soul-do-you-have/

www.ingramcontent.com/pod-product-compliance
Lightning Source LLC
Chambersburg PA
CBHW071901090426
42811CB00004B/700